MORE
PRECIOUS
THAN RUBIES

S. Dilworth Young

MORE PRECIOUS THAN RUBIES

Bookcraft
Salt Lake City, Utah

First Paperback Printing, 1990

Dedication

For Lee A. Palmer

His contributions to, and love for, the boys of the Church
cannot be measured.

Introduction

This book is written with the hope that boys of the Church may gain a better understanding of their Priesthood and its meaning in their lives.

S. Dilworth Young

Contents

CHAPTER 1 •

YOU RECEIVE THE AARONIC PRIESTHOOD

You are a member of the Church of Jesus Christ of Latter-day Saints. If you are a young man, or a boy twelve years of age, you may be given the Aaronic Priesthood. It is conferred upon you by a simple ceremony. Hands are laid on your head and someone with proper authority says, "I confer upon you the Priesthood of Aaron, and ordain you a deacon." He also mentions the fact that he does it because he has authority.

You don't feel much different after the ceremony. This Priesthood is not something you can reach out and touch. Yet because of this ordination you have now a strange new feeling of belonging, and of being a part of the living, vital Church. With new pride you come to meeting to pass the Sacrament for the first time. If you do your work well, that "new feeling" will stay with you always. I still have it whenever I do something worth while for the Church. The feeling is one of deep satisfaction, and is ever fresh.

As you look about you, perhaps you will notice some differences between you and other boys. If you have a friend who does not belong to the Church you will rapidly discover that he doesn't feel the same way about his church as you do about yours. He will not feel the necessity of going to Priesthood meeting because he has no Priesthood meeting that he can attend. He takes no active part in the services, so his interest cannot be as great. He may go because his folks go, or he may stay home, or go fishing; but usually he will not feel impelled (feel the necessity) to go. It will usually be a "take it or leave it" proposition. Not so with you! After you are ordained, provided you try to do right, that impelling feeling will always be with you.

9

You may ask why your friend doesn't have the Priesthood, why he doesn't have things to do each Sunday. You might ask yourself, too, why you do have the Priesthood. Have boys always been able to have it, or have men only? If you were interested in King Arthur and his Knights of the Round Table you might ask, "Did knights have the Priesthood in the days of chivalry?" But as you ask it you will know they did not!

Everybody in the Church knows that the restoration of the Gospel through revelations to the prophet Joseph Smith is the basic reason why you have the Aaronic Priesthood. You have been told the very words which were spoken when John the Baptist placed his hands on Joseph Smith and Oliver Cowdery. Perhaps these words didn't mean much to you then because you didn't know what he meant when he said:

> Upon you my fellow servants, in the name of Messiah I confer the Priesthood of Aaron, which holds the keys of the ministering of angels, and of the gospel of repentance, and of baptism by immersion for the remission of sins . . . (Doc. & Cov. Section 13)

Do you know what is meant by keys? If this Priesthood holds the keys of these three things, how do you turn the key to open things to you?

Let us talk together about how it all came about, and why it is so.

CHAPTER 2 •

OUR RELATION TO GOD, OUR FATHER

You and I know that God lives. At every fast and testi‑ mony meeting you will hear many people say they know that God lives, and that Jesus is the Christ. To know this for yourself is the most important thing you will learn in this life. Jesus Christ, the Lord, acknowledged this when he prayed to his Father the night before he was crucified. We like to quote it as our objective for our whole life's work:

> And this is life eternal, that they might know thee the only true God, and Jesus Christ, whom thou hast sent. (John 17:3)

People ask: "How does one get life eternal?" And we reply: "You must know the true God, his Son, Jesus Christ, and their relation to you."

That is why Joseph Smith was such a great prophet. God our Father favored Joseph Smith with a personal visit when he appeared with his Son Jesus Christ. By showing himself and his Son to Joseph Smith, the Father made it possible for Joseph to bear his testimony that he KNEW that God lives — and that Jesus Christ is indeed the Beloved Son of God. Now let me test your ability to understand plain English:

> God, who at sundry times and in divers manners spake in times past unto the fathers by the prophets,
>
> Hath in these last days spoken unto us by his Son, whom he hath appointed heir of all things, by whom also he made the worlds;
>
> Who being the brightness of his glory, and the *express image of his person,* . . . sat down on the right hand of the Majesty on high; (Hebrews 1:1-3)

I have italicized one phrase. Do you believe it? I am sure it is true.

When you are older you will meet men who will tell you that the words you have just read cannot mean what they say. For 1800 years men have considered God to be an essence, a spirit without form, with no understandable shape. Most Christian people believe as these men seem to believe. They say: "God cannot have a form like man's, for he fills all space. He cannot have a body like ours, for he dwells in our hearts" — so they argue. If you were a member of another church you would argue the same way.

Suppose you were a member of another church and believed that we cannot know God in person. Then if someone like Joseph Smith should come to your meeting and suddenly say, "I know better. I have seen God. He does have a body. It is pure and glorious, but it is in the same form as is man's," it is likely that you might not believe him.

Joseph Smith saw the Father and the Son. He saw that they were alike in looks but were actually two different person-alities. This was a great privilege. In all history it has never been recorded that these great Beings revealed themselves to any-one at the same time. But they chose Joseph Smith for this great honor. He saw them. So he knew — he had seen.

When a person knows, as Joseph Smith knew, that God is a distinct person, then the scriptures make logical sense to him when he reads about God and his dealings with men. The verse you just read sounds right because you know the truth about God and his Son Jesus Christ.

Just to test yourself on your ability to understand, borrow your father's Bible (or better yet, get one of your own) and read these verses:

Exodus 33:9-11.
Numbers 12:7-8.
Acts 7:55-56.

These verses will sound right too, and for the same reason.

Since God is our Father, and we, therefore, are his children, he must have placed us on earth for a reason. He expects some-thing of us. He wants us to seek after and to know him and gain life eternal. He wants us to do it his way — in the manner that he established. He restored his Church 1800 years after it had been taken from the earth, and he re-established his Priesthood. He wants us to learn how to become like him. Re-ceiving and using the Priesthood is the way that he wants us to learn about him and his glory.

He is perfect. He called this power and its use by the name of "The Priesthood after the Order of the Son of God." If you and I are ever to become perfect we must learn to under-stand his power and authority — his Priesthood. He has provided that we may learn to do so, but he does not give us the whole power at once. If he did we would not know how to use it, and it might be dangerous to us.

For example: Let us assume that our Heavenly Father in-spired the modern jet airplane. Such planes in experimental stages have reached a speed as high as 1200 miles per hour — at altitudes so high we can hardly conceive of them. He didn't give this ability to mankind all at once. First, men began by watching birds fly. They noticed that small birds could often go as fast as large ones. They also noticed that some birds such as vultures, hawks, and eagles, soared to great heights without flapping a wing. Then men began to fly kites. They could figure the air resistance which kept a kite up. Later all of this observation was combined and bolder men experimented with gliders. After a time of study and thinking men were ready, and the Wright Brothers applied power — with an engine — to the glider. Then engines were improved, and later the gliders themselves were streamlined. Finally someone got the idea for jet propulsion—and we have jets—and the end is not yet. The knowledge of how to do all this has been slowly accumulating for a long time. If we had it all at once jets would have been dangerous. Now I am sure that the inspiration for the various ideas of airplane development came from God, our Father. But the *push* to get the airplane to develop came from men to whom God gave the principles.

So it is with the Priesthood. We are in the kite stage when we are deacons, but when we are perfect we shall far exceed jets. He will give us the power as we develop. But we must supply the desire and the "push," the "steam," the "flight fuel" ourselves. This fuel is our desire to be like him and our willingness to take part in his work.

CHAPTER 3 •

WHY WE NEED REVELATION

To know that God our Father is an exalted man gives us hope. We can understand that it is possible for him to be our Father. We were told by the Lord Jesus Christ to pray to him as our Father. Jesus himself constantly referred to his Father and said that he did the works his Father commanded him to do.

Before the Lord God revealed himself to Joseph Smith men could not understand how they could be children of a God who had no form and filled all space. So men tried to solve such a mystery by speculating as to his form and being. Most of them did not believe that we lived before we were born on earth. It is impossible to know about that without revelation from God. Men have had a difficult time in trying to find out about the nature of God without revelation.

Let us suppose that when you were born, and before you ever saw your father or your mother, you were placed in the bottom of a deep canyon. By your side were water and food — so you grew. The canyon walls were too steep to climb, and you could not walk out — so you were confined with no escape that you could know. You didn't want to escape anyhow, be-cause you didn't know there was anything better than what you had. How could you know? There would be no one to tell you.

All you could see as you grew was a tree halfway up the canyon wall on a ledge. You could see the sun as it passed over— from about 11 a.m. to 2 p.m., and that was all. You had no way of knowing what was on either side at the top, nor did you know how you got into the canyon in the first place. There you were.

But your father doesn't want to leave you in ignorance. He wants you to learn. He will tell you how you can climb the wall of the canyon and eventually get out — if you are willing to listen. But you don't know that he is your father. All you can hear is his voice as he calls down to you.

So he says: "Son, up here on my side is a great city where people like you live in happiness."

You shout back, "Who are you?"

He answers, "I am your father."

You are liable to say, "Oh, yeah?" But you might also say, "Tell me more."

He would say, "See that tree on the cliff?"

You'd say, "Yes."

He'd reply, "There are millions of them up here."

Now unless your father told you, you'd never know anything about how you got where you are, or why you are there, or how to get where he is. You couldn't know that the sun rises and sets with beautiful sky tints. You couldn't know about mountains, or plains, or rivers, or oceans, or farms, or people. But you could find out if your father kept calling down to you the truth of what he saw on the plateau.

If he told you and you didn't believe him but tried to figure out what he looks like and what that ball of fire is like which passes over every noon, you'd have a tough time ever arriving at the truth.

You and I are like the boy in the bottom of the canyon. We can see the world in which we live, but we need our Father in heaven to call down to us the truth about the world up on top — and to tell us how we got in the world below in the first place — and why we were placed there — and what he expects of us.

For reasons we don't know, the Father did not call down into the canyon to his children during the past 1800 years. When the time came he chose Joseph Smith to be the one to hear his voice, and to tell us what he heard. Joseph Smith heard many things. If he had revealed nothing more than how we lived before we were born, he would have been a great prophet.

CHAPTER 4 •

BEFORE BIRTH

There are many truths which the Lord has revealed to us which give us joy. One of these concerns our life before we were born. Thinking men — serious adults who were real students and wanted to discover — have asked the question of themselves: Who, what, and where, was I before I was born?

To know the answer to that gives reason for our very lives, our hopes, our desire to progress. Men have had many theories about it, and some have concluded that we must have been alive, but the majority have concluded that no one knows, and that life begins at birth on earth. That is what most Christian churches have taught.

They have had a hard time explaining some things which the Lord revealed to prophets in the Bible. For example, the Lord told Jeremiah that he knew him before he was born, and ordained him to be a prophet. (Jeremiah 1:5) That ought to be plain enough, but instead of believing it, they tried to explain it away.

But on May 6, 1833, the Lord Jesus Christ revealed the relationship of himself to his Father, God — and he also declared that "Ye were also in the beginning with the Father." He seemed to want to make it clear that "ye" meant everybody, for he said a few moments later, "Man was also in the beginning with God." Incidentally, at this same time he told us that if we will forsake our sins, and call upon his holy name, and obey his voice, and keep his commandments, we shall see his face — and know not only that he is indeed the Lord, but what his whole relation' ship is to his Father. (Doc. & Cov., Section 93)

He told his disciples that he came down from heaven. They doubted him, not fully understanding. So he asked them a question which seems to be a rebuke. It is as though he said:

18

"You are surprised that I say I came down from heaven. How surprised you will be when you see me ascend up where I was before!"

Brave, loyal Peter finally acknowledged what we all must acknowledge in the end, ". . . Thou hast the words of eternal life. And we believe and are sure that thou art Christ, the Son of the Living God." (John 6:68-69)

CHAPTER 5 •

WHY WE ARE HERE

If we lived happily with our Father in Heaven, and were pleasing to him, why did we leave such a joyful place and come to the earth? These are very vital questions to us. Scientists and philosophers have often pointed out that the main difference between men and animals is that men can think — that they can reason. Some animals can think and reason to a limited extent, but apparently only man has the unlimited ability to do so. A great quality in man is his urgent desire to find out why things should be so. We know that this quality was given to him by his Father — his Eternal Father. As you get older you will ask *Why?* Not now, perhaps, but later. And you will not be happy until you find some answers which will satisfy you.

If you are a Latter-day Saint you will be happy with what is given you by revelation — not always completely satisfied, but happy. So far as your knowledge will go, it will be true, and satisfying. If you are a good member you will constantly strive to learn more. But now let us see what we can know at present.

The Lord gave us his main reason for our spiritual and earthly birth in a great revelation given to Lehi, who told it to his son Jacob. He said this:

> Adam fell that men might be, and men are that they might have joy. (2 Nephi 2:25)

Note that he said that "men are that they might have joy."
Then he went on to say that the Messiah (Jesus Christ) frees us
from original sin so that we are responsible only for our own acts.
And he said, too, that men are free. Thus, God gave us freedom
that we might learn to have joy.

In another revelation he told why he did this great and
marvelous thing:

> For behold, this is my work and my glory — to bring to pass
> the immortality and eternal life of man. (Moses 1:39)

That is saying more than we can understand in one short
sentence. The *chief* purpose of the Father, then, is to give us
eternal life, to the end that we might have joy. This revealed
purpose will come to mean more to you as you get older and
practice the teachings of the Gospel.

The Lord had a plan — a method by which he would do
these great things. He showed to Abraham how he went about
doing this:

> Now the Lord had shown unto me, Abraham, the intelligences
> that were organized before the world was; and among all these there
> were many of the noble and great ones;
>
> And God saw these souls that they were good, and he stood
> in the midst of them, and he said: These I will make my rulers; for
> he stood among those that were spirits, and he saw that they were
> good; and he said unto me: Abraham, thou art one of them; thou
> wast chosen before thou wast born.
>
> And there stood one among them that was like unto God, and
> he said unto those who were with him: We will go down, for there
> is space there, and we will take of these materials, and we will make
> an earth whereon these may dwell;
>
> And we will prove them herewith, to see if they will do all
> things whatsoever the Lord their God shall command them;
>
> And they who keep their first estate shall be added upon; and
> they who keep not their first estate shall not have glory in the same
> kingdom with those who keep their first estate; and they who keep
> their second estate shall have glory added upon their heads for ever
> and ever.
>
> And the Lord said: Whom shall I send? And one answered
> like unto the Son of Man: Here am I, send me. And another
> answered and said: Here am I, send me. And the Lord said: I will
> send the first.
>
> And the second was angry, and kept not his first estate; and,
> at that day, many followed after him. (Abraham 3:22-28)

So he sent us to earth to see which of us would do *all* things whatsoever we were commanded. That is important to us because he must also have an orderly way with which to keep us informed of his desires and a pattern by which we can practice what he wants. "If any man will do my will" is his promise — but how do we know his will?

CHAPTER 6 •

THE PLAN HE MADE TO TEST US

On page 20 you read a quotation from a revelation given to Abraham. This told in a few sentences how Jesus Christ, the Lord, and Lucifer (Satan) each offered to organize the earth and offer the people the plan of God the Father.

You read how the Father accepted the offer of Christ ("I will send the first") and how Lucifer (the second) rebelled. From then on we have been subject to two influences:

1. The influence of Christ to teach us to become perfect through freedom of choice.

2. The influence of Satan to prevent this and eventually to gain control over us himself.

The method which Christ uses to achieve his purpose is to organize his Church, his Kingdom. He states the method by which a person may join the Church, and gives rules which will guide a person in his life so he can stay in it. He warns of evils which, if practiced, will result in the person's being expelled from the Church. He promises eternal life if a person will stand faithful and true to the end. He operates the Church with righteous men as its leaders, and the members take an active place in that leadership. The authority to do this he gives by revelation to prophets, who in turn pass proper authority to those who help. This authority is the Priesthood. One who holds it may serve as called.

On the other hand, Satan tries to prevent this by deception. He tries to convince men that God is different from what we know him to be, that it doesn't matter about the Church — any church will do. He deceives men into believing they are called when they are not truly called.

He does his best to influence them to commit sin, to do wrong things so they will forfeit their right to receive the Holy Ghost. Once they have no guidance from heaven and they feel full of despair, he persuades them that they might just as well keep on sinning — they've lost their chance now anyhow. He uses lies and deception to achieve his ends. And those who follow him eventually do the same things to achieve theirs.

You can easily keep out of the influence of Satan by deciding to follow the Gospel of Christ. You are given the Priesthood to help you learn of the power of God, and to help others to learn.

It is like being made a member of the team. The team is united, every player doing his part, and yet not interfering with, but rather helping, the other players to do their parts. It's fun to play to win on a team like that.

When you are not a member of the team you are on the side lines, or in the grandstand. You can see the team playing, but you cannot know what is said in the huddle before each play, nor can you have the thrill of carrying the ball, or blocking the opposition.

When you have the Priesthood given to you, you are in the huddle, you hear the plays called, you suggest plays yourself, and occasionally you yourself make a touchdown. You take the penalties when you break the rules or get off side, but you are on the winning team, playing to win the greatest game on earth— life eternal!

CHAPTER 7 •

HOW REVELATION IS RECEIVED

To receive revelation from the Lord God is the most exciting and satisfying experience that can come to man. There are men on earth who seek excitement by hunting wild animals. There are others who satisfy this craving by living lives of danger and adventure. Climbing Mt. Everest certainly was a desperate, dangerous adventure. The experience of Admiral Byrd when he stayed alone near the South Pole for several months, nearly losing his life in the process, was an exciting, desperate gamble with the elements. A few days ago I read in the newspaper that a certain officer is to fly a plane so high that he will be almost out of the air envelope which surrounds the earth. His plane will have to be launched from a "mother plane" which will take him up to 40,000 feet before he starts. Practice flights to that point were being made. That is thrilling. Still — none of these is as exciting, as satisfying as receiving revelation. Man

23

seek thrills by going into the unknown. The greatest unknowns are the world from which we came and the paradise to which we will go after we leave the earth. Our only way to learn about them is by revelation until, of course, we actually go there.

Back in 1916 there sailed from England, bound for New York, the fastest ship of its day — the Titanic. It was advertised as unsinkable. Many famous people were on it to have the adventure of breaking the record for time in crossing the Atlantic. But the Titanic struck an iceberg. It didn't take long for the ship to fill up with water, and it sank very rapidly. The sailors through heroic effort got most of the women and children into the lifeboats but many men were drowned. Charles Frohman and a friend were on deck waiting their turn for rescue — if there should be room in one of the boats. Mr. Frohman was calm in the face of his crisis. He remarked to his friend, "The greatest adventure in life is death." And so it appears. But learning about our past before birth, our future after we leave here, and being warned of events in our own lives while here are greater still.

The Lord God reveals his purpose and his desires to men. He gives the righteous satisfying knowledge about themselves. He calls down to us in our deep canyon of ignorance and tells us what to expect when we climb out onto the plateau above. The key to his intentions and his method of operation is given to us in a declaration made by a Prophet named Amos. You will want to remember what he said. This will be easy to do, for the statement is very short. This is it:

> Surely the Lord God will do nothing, but he revealeth his secret unto his servants the prophets. (Amos 3:7)

This statement is true. The Lord has revealed his plan, his purpose in sending us to earth, our future after leaving, and he has given us warnings of events before they have taken place. He has chosen faithful men to receive the messages to be delivered to the people. These men are known as prophets. Several methods are used in delivering these important messages:

1. By personal visitation of Jesus Christ the Lord himself.

You already know about the first vision to Joseph Smith in a grove of trees in New York State. Here is the account of how the Brother of Jared received a message from Christ long before the Lord was born in Bethlehem:

And it came to pass that when the brother of Jared had said these words, behold, the Lord stretched forth his hand and touched the stones one by one with his finger. And the veil was taken from off the eyes of the brother of Jared, and he saw the finger of the Lord; and it was as the finger of man, like unto flesh and blood; and the brother of Jared fell down before the Lord, for he was struck with fear.

And the Lord saw that the brother of Jared had fallen to the earth; and the Lord said unto him: Arise, why hast thou fallen?

And he saith unto the Lord: I saw the finger of the Lord, and I feared lest he should smite me; for I knew not that the Lord had flesh and blood.

And the Lord said unto him: Because of thy faith thou hast seen that I shall take upon me flesh and blood; and never has man come before me with such exceeding faith as thou hast; for were it not so ye could not have seen my finger. Sawest thou more than this?

And he answered: Nay; Lord, show thyself unto me.

And the Lord said unto him: Believest thou the words which I shall speak?

And he answered: Yea, Lord, I know that thou speaketh the truth, for thou art a God of truth, and canst not lie.

And when he had said these words, behold, the Lord showed himself unto him, and said: Because thou knowest these things ye are redeemed from the fall; therefore ye are brought back into my presence; therefore I show myself unto you.

Behold, I am he who was prepared from the foundation of the world to redeem my people. Behold, I am Jesus Christ. I am the Father and the Son. In me shall all mankind have light, and that eternally, even they who shall believe on my name; and they shall become my sons and my daughters.

And never have I showed myself unto man whom I have created, for never has man believed in me as thou hast. Seest thou that ye are created after mine own image? Yea, even all men were created in the beginning after mine own image.

Behold, this body, which ye now behold, is the body of my spirit; and man have I created after the body of my spirit; and even as I appear unto thee to be in the spirit will I appear unto my people in the flesh. (Ether 3:6-16)

2. By angelic messengers.

There have been innumerable angelic messengers sent to the people of the covenant. You can read of them in the Bible. In our day a glorious visitation was made to Joseph Smith in the Kirtland Temple. At this time he was given three of the great keys of the Priesthood.

> After this vision closed, the heavens were again opened unto us; and Moses appeared before us, and committed unto us the keys of the gathering of Israel from the four parts of the earth, and the leading of the ten tribes from the land of the north.
>
> After this, Elias appeared, and committed the dispensation of the gospel of Abraham, saying that in us and our seed, all generations after us should be blessed.
>
> After this vision had closed, another great and glorious vision burst upon us; for Elijah the prophet, who was taken to heaven without tasting death, stood before us, and said:
>
> Behold, the time has fully come, which was spoken of by the mouth of Malachi — testifying that he [Elijah] should be sent, before the great and dreadful day of the Lord come —
>
> To turn the hearts of the fathers to the children, and the children to the fathers, lest the whole earth be smitten with a curse —·
>
> Therefore, the keys of this dispensation are committed into your hands; and by this ye may know that the great and dreadful day of the Lord is near, even at the doors. (Doc. and Cov. 110:11-16)

These were three angelic messengers sent at the same time. Did you notice that the first line starts out with these words, "After this vision closed"? If you care as some boys do, you will want to know what vision. You can easily learn about that if you desire by reading the first eleven verses in Section 110 of the Doctrine and Covenants — Your folks have a copy.

3. By the inspiration of the Holy Ghost.

By far the greatest amount of revelation comes by this method. This is the means by which the Lord guides us daily, and gives his prophets their words to speak.

The President of the Church, who is a prophet, daily receives promptings of the Spirit of the Holy Ghost in his efforts to guide the Church affairs. The president of your stake receives this guidance in handling stake affairs. Your bishop is constantly inspired likewise in making appointments in the ward, in advising people when they consult him, and in making decisions. All your life you will be thrilled, too, by the stories you hear from returning missionaries. This one will illustrate how inspiration came to two of them:

Two elders, working without purse or scrip (without money), were walking down a country road. They passed a house but did not go to it to deliver their message. After they passed they began to feel uneasy. The farther they walked the worse they felt. After about a mile they stopped and looked at each other. One said, "Maybe we'd better go back to that house." So they went. They knocked at the door. When the housewife opened it she said, "I saw you pass and I hoped you would stop, for I wanted to hear your message. I was disappointed when you passed by without coming in." Her husband wanted to hear the message too. Those two joined the Church. As a result there is a thriving branch of the Church in that community. In that case the spirit was manifest by making the elders uneasy. Then the idea was planted in their minds that they ought to go to that house.

On the day you were confirmed into the Church you were given the Holy Ghost. This great gift is yours from that day as long as you are righteous. If you can learn to understand it, it will guide you in your life. You will be informed, warned of danger. Future events in your life will be revealed.

Joseph Smith said an exciting thing when he stated that if man had the Holy Ghost he would prophesy, for the spirit of the Holy Ghost is the spirit of prophecy. You will be able to prophesy — not about the Church, or the future of the world — but about your own personal affairs, so in a sense you can become a prophet of God. Indeed, it is expected that you will become one, for you as a Priesthood bearer are expected to live so that you can receive the whisperings of the Holy Ghost.

It will take you some time to recognize these whisperings, but if you are obedient in your work in the Priesthood and keep the commandments, obeying your parents and being kind, you will come to know the guidance of the Holy Ghost. You will never experience any greater joy in your whole life than you will when the spirit of the Holy Ghost is given you to show you the path you should take.

CHAPTER 8 •

HOW PROPHETS COME TO BE PROPHETS

If the Lord God will do nothing unless he reveals his will to his prophets, the question will arise in your mind, "How does he call or designate who is to be a prophet?"

We know very well how he does *not* call men to be prophets. He does not give his authority to men who call themselves. One of the sure signs that the minister of a church has no authority to speak to the people is that he *felt* called to be a minister. Another sign is that the salary to be paid very often is the controlling factor as to which location he will accept. In that situation a congregation "calls" him. And so it does — but not the Lord. This does not mean that such a man is not sincere, or that he is not a good man. Some of the most Christlike men on earth are these self-called men. But they are not called of God. They mistake their desire to represent God for a call from God. Paul the Apostle tells how this really was done. Speaking of the Priesthood which truly represents God he said:

> And no man taketh this honor unto himself, but he that is called of God, as was Aaron. (Hebrews 5:4)

This should make you curious to know how Aaron was called. He was great enough to hold the keys to the Aaronic Priesthood and to have it called after his name. He was called by Moses, through revelation of God. Moses himself was called by the Lord God. Remember the story of the burning bush? We shall not take time to recount it here, but the story of Aaron's call is in Exodus, chapter 28. You will find the Lord's instruction to Moses in Exodus, chapter 4.

Let us discover how three of the prophets were called. We know they were true prophets.

1. *Isaiah*:

Also, I heard the voice of the Lord, saying, Whom shall I send, and who will go for us? Then said I, Here am I, send me.

And he said, Go, and tell this people, Hear ye indeed, but understand not; and see ye indeed, but perceive not. (Isaiah 6:8-9)

2. *Jeremiah*:

Then the word of the Lord came unto me, saying,

Before I formed thee in the belly I knew thee; and before thou camest out of the womb I sanctified thee, and I ordained thee a prophet unto the nations.

Then said I, Ah, Lord God! behold, I cannot speak: for I am a child.

But the Lord said unto me, Say not, I am a child: for thou shalt go to all that I shall send thee, and whatsoever I command thee thou shalt speak. (Jeremiah 1:4-7)

3. *Ezekiel*:

And he said unto me, Son of man, stand upon thy feet, and I will speak unto thee.

And the spirit entered into me when he spake unto me, and set me upon my feet, that I heard him that spake unto me.

And he said unto me, Son of man, I send thee to the children of Israel, to a rebellious nation that hath rebelled against me: . . And thou shalt speak my words unto them . . . (Ezekiel 2:1-3, 7)

From what Jeremiah said it is clear that prophets to the nations of the world are chosen in the spirit world before they are born on earth, and the times of their coming to earth are chosen also. Then the Lord reveals himself to that person, calls him, and sends him forth to speak in the name of the Lord. The following scripture bears this out:

. . . Abraham, thou art one of them; thou wast chosen before thou wast born. (Abraham 3:23)

Now what do you think of Joseph Smith? He was one of the greatest of all prophets and was reserved to be the prophet of this last dispensation. Is it any wonder that, when the Lord decided the time had come to restore his Church, he and his Father came and revealed themselves to Joseph so that he could, having seen with his eyes, declare anew the nature and being of God?

Joseph Smith became a Prophet of God because the Lord God personally called him.

You and I have the true Priesthood to represent the Lord because we in our turn were called by men ordained and called by the Prophet of God, just as Aaron was called.

CHAPTER 9 •

WHY THERE IS A PRIESTHOOD

We shall be happy and contented to be members of our quorum and do our share of quorum assignments because we have an understanding of the purposes of our Father in heaven in relation to us. This is a very important means by which we learn to have joy and to serve him. Each variety of experience makes us better prepared to meet him when the time comes. We can be happy that we hold the Priesthood.

Boys of other churches often envy the close-knit companionship of boys in quorums of the Priesthood. Their leaders place them in social organizations to get this feeling of belonging. But our boys could well ask them: "A feeling of belonging to 'what'?" Not knowing just what "what" is, leads to a dead end. But you *know,* so you are that much ahead.

Let us ask the question, "Why is there a Priesthood?" We could give many reasons. We can imagine that we are in the place of the Lord. He looks about and sees his children. He wants them to be "official." So he says in effect, "I will give each boy the official right to be my assistant on earth. Then when he has a right to be my 'official assistant' I shall assign him jobs and responsibilities. The responsibilities will be the offices to which he will be ordained, and the 'jobs' will be the specific tasks and items which he will be doing at any one time."

He then gives us the Aaronic Priesthood. This makes us his official assistants. Then he ordains us to the office of a deacon, or a teacher, or a priest. This gives us our field of responsibility. Then he has us pass the Sacrament, which is a job to be done in the field of our responsibility. While we are growing up we can learn how to work in three fields of responsibility. Each has its own kind of jobs to be done:

1. *Deacons* — Office of Responsibility:
   a. Passing the Sacrament.
   b. Collecting the Fast offerings.
   c. Being messengers at Sacrament meeting.
2. *Teachers* — Office of Responsibility:
   a. Passing the Sacrament.
   b. Ward teaching.
3. *Priests* — Office of Responsibility:
   a. Preparing the Sacrament.
   b. Administering (blessing) the Sacrament.
   c. Passing the Sacrament.
   d. Ward teaching.
   e. Missionary work (preaching and teaching.)
   f. Baptizing converts and children.

Notice that the teacher can take responsibility in the deacon's field and that the priest can take responsibility in the teacher's and deacon's fields. There are other jobs which can be added to those listed.

Of course, this is the way we have imagined it could be. Actually the Priesthood is something bigger than just being assigned to be a representative. It is an eternal power. While God uses it as his authority, he does so because he has it in perfection.

It is a tangible power which can be evoked to do other things when we are old enough and have learned enough. The power of the Priesthood is the power of God. He gives it to us; then we spend our lives learning how to evoke it, how to apply it, how to use it. So it is not only the appointment to be a "helper to God," but it is also permission to start to learn to use the power by which God operates his Church, his Kingdom, and this world.

If we are to become like him — perfect — then we must start somewhere to obey his laws and use his power. It is like learning to run the family car. We practice until we can control the power and move the car as we will. We don't learn over-night, but we do learn if we start and keep at it until we understand how to operate it.

You may learn to drive a car in a week, but it will take a long time for you to be able to meet every situation and a lot longer time for you to know why the gasoline when mixed with air and fired by a spark develops enough power to lift the car over the high mountain pass at the head of Parley's Canyon east of Salt Lake City — remembering that the car weighs more than a ton, while the gasoline to do the job weighs about eight pounds.

Here is a problem for you:

You step on the gas and the car climbs the hill. You see it happen. You can measure the amount of gas burned.

Now on the other hand, your father and a friend lay their hands on your sick brother and command the disease to depart by the "power of the Priesthood." Do you know how much power that is? Can you measure it in quarts or gallons? No, you cannot. You will spend your whole life, if you are faithful, learning the answer to that problem. There will be times that you will "feel" the power. It can make you weak or it can make you doubly strong.

Believe me, it is worth working for, just to experience this power once. Faithful members experience it many times.

CHAPTER 10

THE PRIESTHOOD AND THE KEYS

Boys—and girls too—have many privileges when they are members of the Church. They take part in many activities. The Sunday School, the Mutual Improvement Association, and the Primary all provide programs of activity and interest which are given to all, regardless of the offices they may hold. For example, you can play on the basketball team, if you are capable enough, or be in the roadshow, or go to camp with the scouts. You may also cut the ward lawn or paint woodwork in the meetinghouse. These things have to do with you and your normal earthly existence.

But there are some activities in which you take part which are prescribed by the Lord. These have to do with handling his spiritual kingdom. He governs both the earthly activities and the spiritual activities by the use of men and boys holding the Priesthood. The difference is that you can be invited to take part in any of the earthly activities with or without holding the Priesthood, while you cannot take part in the spiritual direction of the Church unless you do hold the Priesthood. (In the women's organizations women are given keys of presidency without holding the Priesthood.)

No boy does anything in the Priesthood work of the Church unless he is asked or "called" to do it. Holding the Priesthood, then, gives him an unending privilege to be asked — to be called — to do certain things. These things may be given to him in two ways:

1. They may have been assigned by the Lord.
2. They may have been assigned by the President of the Church or by his bishop.

If they are assigned by the Lord, no one can change them unless told to do so in a revelation.

Here's one that was assigned by the Lord:

> Upon you my fellow servants, in the name of Messiah I confer the Priesthood of Aaron, which holds the keys of the ministering of angels, and of the gospel of repentance, and of baptism by immersion for the remission of sins; and this shall never be taken again from the earth, until the sons of Levi do offer again an offering unto the Lord in righteousness. (Doc. & Cov. Section 13)

Notice that among other things the Lord said (through John the Baptist, of course) that the Aaronic Priesthood holds the keys of baptism.

Now here is another one:

> The priest's duty is to preach, teach, expound, exhort, and baptize, and administer the sacrament, . . . (Doc. & Cov. 20:46)

This specifies that a priest may baptize, but can teachers and deacons?

> But neither teachers nor deacons have authority to baptize, administer the sacrament, or lay on hands; . . . (Doc. & Cov. 20:58)

Thus we are told that teachers or deacons may not baptize.

These are examples in which the Lord gives the Aaronic Priesthood to each one, and then limits each office as to what the one holding it may do. So if you are a holder of the Aaronic Priesthood you are limited in what you may do. The assignment is given by your bishop. He may change it or relieve you of it. The one who holds the power to assign when directing you may fit the job to your ability.

THE KEYS

The fact that you have a right to be asked implies that someone has the right to ask you. A man with such a right is said to hold the "keys." He has authority to direct you and preside over you.

The President of the Church has all of the keys that exist on earth. They were given to him by the Lord. He can direct anyone in the Church. He may do one of two things:

1. He may give a key to a man to direct others. Examples of this are stake presidents and bishops.
2. He may direct another to do a certain task. This man may be asked to write a magazine article, or to investi-

34

gate a piece of land which is being considered for purchase.

The President of the Church has given your bishop the keys of presiding over your ward. The bishop can, in his turn, give keys of presidency to leaders of ward organizations. In this he is the representative of the President of the Church. So he calls the officers of the Sunday School, M.I.A., Primary, and Relief Society. He calls the boys who preside over your quorum. He gives to each the specific keys of that organization.

The man who was appointed by the President of the Church to write a magazine article or to look at some land was not given a "key." He cannot pass his job on to someone else. He must do it himself. He can *accept* the assignment but he *cannot pass it on*. Teachers of classes are limited in this manner. They cannot pass the assignment on. You are like him, too, when you are assigned to pass the Sacrament next Sunday, or to go to Jones' house for fast offerings, or to administer the Sacrament. You have no authority to get someone to take your place. You are required to do the assignment yourself.

Were it not for this system of authorities, keys, assignments, and obedience to the system, the Church would soon be torn with argument and confusion. As it is, there is perfect order. Each one has assignments received from certain others who hold keys — or authorities — to give the assignment. These certain others receive their keys through a direct line to the President of the Church — and he is the one to whom the Lord looks for the direction of his earthly work.

In no other church on earth is there such harmony and willing obedience to this heavenly and inspired order. You will work in it all your days. If you are faithful you will have the opportunity to hold keys and preside, as well as to obey those who hold keys and preside. Truly it has been said that until one has learned to be obedient he cannot preside well and persuade others to obey him. Later on you will learn that the Lord himself was perfectly obedient to his Father — thus justifying his appoint' ment as Creator of the World.

CHAPTER 11 •

THE TWO PRIESTHOODS

Suppose your father gave you the use of a new car, and you drove it. In the process you felt grown up, important, and were inclined to show off. So you exceeded the speed limit, ran a couple of red lights, hugged the center line and occasionally crossed it slightly to scare drivers coming from the opposite direction. You were arrested several times, and finally lost your license. So your father took the car away from you and bought you a bicycle. It had wheels and you could go faster than you could run, but you were curtailed in your power.

In a crude sort of way this supposition illustrates the way in which the chosen people received the Aaronic Priesthood.

For reasons best known to himself, the Lord selected Abraham to be the progenitor of his chosen family. The chosen seed are especially mentioned. Abraham was so faithful that the Lord said that through his seed all the nations of the earth should be blessed. I do not know of a single prophet after his time who was not one of his descendants, including all of the prophets in the Bible and all of the prophets in the Book of Mormon except those of the Jaredites, who came to America before his time. Samuel the Lamanite, Nephi, Lehi, King Benjamin, and the twelve disciples chosen by the Lord on the American continent were all descendants of Abraham. The Lord Jesus Christ, himself, was of the seed of Abraham, as was Joseph Smith.

This prophecy in the Book of Mormon foretells Joseph Smith:

> And thus prophesied Joseph, saying: Behold, that seer will the Lord bless; and they that seek to destroy him shall be confounded; for this promise, which I have obtained of the Lord, of the fruit of my loins, shall be fulfilled. Behold, I am sure of the fulfilling of this promise;

And his name shall be called after me; and it shall be after the name of his father. And he shall be like unto me; for the thing, which the Lord shall bring forth by his hand, by the power of the Lord shall bring my people unto salvation. (2 Nephi 3:14-15)

It is true that many of the descendants of Abraham were not worthy to hold the Priesthood. Like the boy with the car they misused their power. You know well the story of the Israelites [children of Israel. Israel was another name given to Jacob because of his faithfulness], and how they worshipped the golden calf, an idol they made as soon as Moses went up into the mountain. In spite of his greatness Moses could not persuade them to remain true and faithful. They could not seem to understand spiritual things, or spiritual power. They seemed to comprehend only earthly things, things they could see and handle. So the Lord in his mercy withdrew the higher law of the Priesthood from them, and governed them with that part of the Priesthood dealing with the earthly things. Aaron, the brother of Moses, was given the right to preside over this Priesthood forever. It was given his name. As Aaron was less in authority than Moses, so his part of the Priesthood was also less.

With the tribe of the Levites to act as his helpers, Aaron began to administer the law. Because the Levites assisted Aaron, this lesser authority has been known as the Levitical Priesthood. Its authority gave its holders the general right to offer sacrifice, to collect tithes and offerings, to perform baptisms, and to take care of the poor. The operation of this lesser Priesthood was all that the people had until the coming of Jesus Christ. He, of course, brought back the higher Priesthood.

In the ancient times there lived in the land a representative of the Lord by the name of Melchizedek. Very little has been said about him. About all we know is that he was called the King of Salem and that Abraham received the Priesthood from him and paid tithes to him.

Which Abraham received the priesthood from Melchizedek, who received it through the lineage of his fathers, even till Noah; . . . (Doc. & Cov. 84:14)

That he was a favorite son of the Lord is evident because he held the higher Priesthood. We know this, and we know that he was especially honored because when the men of that day sought to avoid the constant repetition of the name of the Son of God, which was the name of the Priesthood, they were told to say "the Melchizedek Priesthood."

Why the first is called the Melchizedek Priesthood is because Melchizedek was such a great high priest.

Before his day it was called *the Holy Priesthood after the Order of the Son of God.*

But out of respect or reverence to the name of the Supreme Being, to avoid the too frequent repetition of his name, they, the church, in ancient days, called that priesthood after Melchizedek, or the Melchizedek Priesthood. (Doc. & Cov. 107:2-4)

You are used to hearing the titles of these divisions of the Priesthood. You hold the Aaronic Priesthood. Many men of your acquaintance hold the Melchizedek Priesthood. You do not give it much thought because it is so common today. You assume without much thinking that when you are old enough you will receive the Melchizedek Priesthood. And you will if you are true and faithful.

CHAPTER 12

YOUR RELATION TO YOUR BISHOP

As a young man growing up into Church responsibility you will do well to know your relation to your bishop. First, however, let us look at a verse from the Doctrine and Covenants:

13. The second priesthood is called the Priesthood of Aaron, because it was conferred upon Aaron and his seed, throughout all their generations.

14. Why it is called the lesser priesthood is because it is an appendage to the greater, or the Melchizedek Priesthood, and has power in administering outward ordinances.

15. The bishopric is the presidency of this priesthood, and holds the keys or authority of the same.

16. No man has a legal right to this office, to hold the keys of this priesthood, except he be a literal descendant of Aaron.

17. But as a high priest of the Melchizedek Priesthood has authority to officiate in all the lesser offices, he may officiate in the office of bishop when no literal descendant of Aaron can be found, provided he is called and set apart and ordained unto this power by the hands of the Presidency of the Melchizedek Priesthood. (Doc. & Cov. 107: 13-17)

Note verse 15 especially. In obedience to the commandment thus stated, the Prophet organized the Presiding Bishopric. These men preside — they hold the keys of presidency — over all of the Aaronic Priesthood. As the Church has grown it has been necessary to make many subdivisions known as wards. And in each ward a bishop has been appointed. He has two counselors. These are not bishops themselves, but they advise him and per-form many duties for him.

The bishop presides over every person in the ward and directs their local church activities. He especially presides over the Aaronic Priesthood. All of your adolescent life you will be under the direction of the bishop. He will appoint teachers and supervisors to do his work, but he will be very much interested in your progress. Your life here will be constantly weighed by him, for he is the judge of your worthiness to advance in the Priest-hood, to receive higher ordinances, and to be worthy to go to the Temple.

If you are going to work in the Church system you will learn to be obedient to your bishop. If you get into trouble you will be wise if you seek his advice and counsel. He has been designated by the Lord and appointed by the President of the Church to be responsible for you and to make sure you progress according to your worthiness and ability.

His responsibilities are many. His duties are so numerous that he cannot possibly perform them all without the willing and complete support of the ward members. You are in a good position to help. No bishop's job is onerous if the boys of the Aaronic Priesthood are back of him. When they are helping and eager about it, his heart will sing, and if he is happy with you, the rest will be easy.

It is here that you first learn and practice loyalty. It is here that you show the Lord (through the bishop) that the reason for your being here — "to see if you will do all things whatsoever the Lord shall command" — is not in vain. Learn this lesson well as a member of the Aaronic Priesthood, and you will be more than half way to your goal.

Many people will not work for the bishop. Will you?

Many people criticize the bishop in his responsible decisions. Do you?

Many stand and support him with all their hearts. Do you?

The bishop will not direct you in everything. He will appoint the best men he can find to teach you the lessons and to give you the assignments. When you are loyal to them you are loyal to him. He will meet you at the important times. He will see you every year at tithing settlement. He will interview you when you are to be ordained to a new office. He will judge when you are worthy to become an elder and will talk to you about it. If you go on a mission he will be the one who makes the first inquiry as to your fitness and ability to serve in this capacity. If you are very sick you will find him standing by your bed more often than anyone but your own family, and should any of your folks die, he will make arrangements for and conduct the funeral.

He does all of this because the Lord commands it and because he loves the people of the ward with a deep affection.

Note 1966: The home teachers do much of this detail work now. They represent the bishop.

CHAPTER 13

YOUR NEED TO LEARN HOW TO USE THE PRIESTHOOD

Once when Joseph Smith was asked how the Church differed from other churches the Prophet replied, "We have the Holy Ghost." He meant something which his listeners did not comprehend.

The Holy Ghost was given to you when you were confirmed a member of the Church after your baptism. It is one of the greatest gifts which is conferred upon new members of the Church. Yet you need to learn how to receive it, how to use it, and how to keep it. You can, and undoubtedly will, grow in knowledge, power, and usefulness because of it. If you will not forfeit it by unrighteous living this great gift will bring you joy unspeakable.

In answer to the question, "How are you different?" the Prophet could easily have said, "We have the Priesthood" — and again they would not have understood. No church, except this one, operates with such a widespread giving and using of its authority. Every man and boy is expected to receive authority and to work in various positions under its appointments. Can you think of any other way that each will have equal opportunity to represent the Lord?

A young man is ignorant of how to apply it or how to use it, yet it is given to him in his ignorance. He does not go through a lengthy school of instruction to become expert in its forms or in its ceremonies. If he makes a mistake, or is awkward in performing some task, no one takes any exception. Everyone knows that with practice smoothness of form will follow. But no one doubts, either, that with it must be sincerity of purpose. You might blunder with words because of fear, but the Lord knows what is in your soul to say, and he understands and accepts.

This Priesthood must become something very personal to you if it is to have meaning. Later on you will apply its principles and ordinances to your own family. You will bless your children, and you will ask God to cure them in illness by its power. You will not want to have to lean on other men for these choice blessings and experiences. Nor will you need to.

Sorry is the family which must wait for the elders in time of great need. Happy is the family where the father can exercise his Priesthood authority at once. You are now in the process of learning to use the Priesthood. But you are also learning to use it in connection with the gift of the Holy Ghost, for there must be inspiration in its use. Each act, each obedience, each assign-ment, is your chance to improve in understanding — "to grow in grace," as we often say.

Joseph Smith was right. If you constantly try to perform well in your assigned tasks, no one will need to ask how we are different. He will see it with his own eyes.

The other day I saw ten young men of almost thirteen years of age walk past my house. They did not march as one unit, but were in groups of two and three. None had coats — the weather was hot. Most had their sleeves rolled up and their shirts open at the throat. They were headed in the general direc-tion of the ward meetinghouse. Since one of my neighbors has a son who is confined to his bed with an illness, I suspected. where they had been.

I said, "Where have you boys been?"

One answered, "We have been to visit with our sick friend."

I asked, "Where are you now going?"

Another replied, "To Sunday School to pass the Sacrament."

They were different from other groups of boys. They had organization; they had purpose; they belonged; they were learn-ing how to use their Priesthood and its power. They had the right — they were ordained to it — and they knew it. They seemed happy — and they were.

43

PRIESTHOOD RESPONSIBILITIES

WHAT THE LORD SAID:	THE BISHOP ASSIGNS DUTIES AS AUTHORIZED IN THE REVELATIONS:	DUTIES ASSIGNED BY THE BISHOP NOT STATED IN THE REVELATIONS:
	## PRIESTS	
Revelation explaining responsibilities of priests: (Doc. & Cov. 20:46-52)	46. The *priest's* duty is to preach, teach, expound, exhort, and baptize, and administer the sacrament, 47. And visit the house of each member, and exhort them to pray vocally and in secret and attend to all family duties. 48. And he may also ordain other priests, teachers, and deacons. 49. And he is to take the lead of meetings when there is no elder present; 50. But when there is an elder present, he is only to preach, teach, expound, exhort, and baptize, 51. And visit the house of each member, exhorting them to pray vocally and in secret and attend to all family duties. 52. In all these duties the priest is to assist the elder if occasion requires.	Hold and attend cottage meetings. Give talks in Church. Be recommended as stake missionaries. Baptize children. Administer the Sacrament. Ordain to the Aaronic Priesthood (when assigned). Take charge of meetings when no elder is present. Do home teaching.	Counselor in an auxiliary. Secretary to organizations. Teacher in organizations. Special assignments.
(Doc. & Cov. 84:111)	111. And behold, the high priests should travel, and also the elders, and also the lesser priests; . . .	While the priests may travel as missionaries, the teachers and deacons may serve only in the ward.	

44

TEACHERS

Revelation explaining responsibilities of teachers: (Doc. & Cov. 20:53-56)

53. The *teacher's* duty is to watch over the church always, and be with and strengthen them;

54. And see that there is no iniquity in the church, neither hardness with each other, neither lying, backbiting, nor evil speaking;

55. And see that the church meet together often, and also see that all members do their duty.

56. And he is to take the lead of meetings in the absence of the elder or priest —

Do home teaching.
Take charge of meetings when no elder or priest is present.

Clean up after Sacrament.
Pass the Sacrament.
Collect Fast Offering envelopes.
Deliver messages.
Prepare Sacrament table.
Do odd jobs in the ward.
Perform welfare assignments.
Usher in meetings.

DEACONS

Revelation explaining responsibilities of deacons: (Doc. & Cov. 20:57)

57. And is to be assisted always, in all his duties in the church, by the *deacons*, if occasion requires.

Assist teachers when occasion requires.

Restrictions placed by the Lord: (Doc. & Cov. 20:58-59)

58. But neither teachers nor deacons have authority to baptize, administer the sacrament, or lay on hands;

59. They are, however, to warn, expound, exhort, and teach, and invite all to come unto Christ.

(The bishop cannot ask teachers or deacons to baptize, administer the Sacrament, or ordain other teachers and deacons.)

(Doc. & Cov. 84:111)

111. ... but the deacons and teachers should be appointed to watch over the church, to be standing ministers unto the church.

While the priests may travel as missionaries, the teachers and deacons may serve only in the ward.

Pass the Sacrament.
Collect Fast Offering envelopes.
Act as messenger for the bishopric at Sacrament meeting.
Fulfill special assignments.

CHAPTER 14 •

SOMETHING EVERY BOY SHOULD KNOW

When I was a boy I didn't know very much about my responsibility in the Priesthood. I imagine you don't either. Times change, but boys don't. You know you have jobs and assignments, for we have talked about that. You know quite generally what these are. We have listed some of them in Chapter 9. As a deacon I went along, doing what I was invited to do. I was sure of only three things:

Deacons pass the Sacrament in the Sunday School.

Teachers pass the Sacrament in the Sacrament Meetings
(occasionally assisted by the deacons).

Priests administer the Sacrament.

When I became a priest the bishop asked me to baptize a child. Thus I learned that a priest baptizes.

There is every reason for you to know what you are really expected to do. The comparative chart on the preceding pages will tell you specifically what the Lord said — and then, opposite each office, what the bishop assigns you to do.

If you study the chart and what the Lord said, you will readily see that when the Lord has not designated or restricted, the bishop may assign any boy to do any job at hand which needs doing. And when the Lord has spoken, then the bishop is restricted in his assignments in conformity with what the Lord has said. So the bishop is obedient to the Presiding Bishopric, and to the Lord. If you looked at the chart you should now know what the Lord expects in a general way, but you will still have to be assigned before you can do the job.

So we can learn that indeed the Lord's Church is one of order, obedience, and voluntary discipline. You have a rare opportunity to learn these fundamental necessities and to practice order, obedience, and voluntary discipline.

CHAPTER 15

THREE KEYS OF THE AARONIC PRIESTHOOD

A person reading in the books of the Old Testament dealing with the Levitical Priesthood and its privileges can get lost in the maze of detail in which the Jews were bound by their belief. Having only this part of the whole Priesthood to guide them they seemed to feel obliged to make a rule to cover every situation.

When John the Baptist came and gave the keys of this work to Joseph Smith and Oliver Cowdery, he simplified things. He gave them three general keys. These cover the whole responsibility of the Aaronic Priesthood. You are given the Aaronic Priesthood. You learned in the last chapter that a priest may do several specific things in the Church. These definite jobs are because you have three specific rights. They are to be put into action as you are called by the authority over you. They include:

1. The ministering of angels.
2. The gospel of repentance.
3. Baptism by immersion for the remission of sins.

Let us discuss each one separately:

First Key — THE MINISTERING OF ANGELS

The most thrilling, because the least exhibited, is the right to receive the ministering of angels. Let's see how this worked in the case of Zacharias (who held this Priesthood).

> And there appeared unto him an angel of the Lord standing on the right side of the altar of incense.
>
> And when Zacharias saw him, he was troubled, and fear fell upon him.

But the angel said unto him, Fear not, Zacharias; for thy prayer is heard; and thy wife Elizabeth shall bear thee a son, and thou shalt call his name John.

And thou shalt have joy and gladness; and many shall rejoice at his birth.

For he shall be great in the sight of the Lord, and shall drink neither wine nor strong drink; and he shall be filled with the Holy Ghost, even from his mother's womb.

And many of the children of Israel shall he turn to the Lord their God.

And he shall go before him in the spirit and power of Elias, to turn the hearts of the fathers to the children, and the disobedient to the wisdom of the just; to make ready a people prepared for the Lord.

And Zacharias said unto the angel, Whereby shall I know this? for I am an old man, and my wife well stricken in years.

And the angel answering said unto him, I am Gabriel, that stand in the presence of God; and am sent to speak unto thee, and to shew thee these glad tidings.

And, behold, thou shalt be dumb, and not able to speak, until the day that these things shall be performed, because thou believest not my words, which shall be fulfilled in their season. (Luke 1:11-20)

A great event was to take place. A great man was to be born who would exercise his right in the Aaronic Priesthood and would be appointed to baptize the Lord Jesus Christ. This message was delivered to Zacharias by an angel, who even announced his name and by whom he was sent.

In his later years Wilford Woodruff said that he had some of the most satisfying experiences of his life while he was a priest on a mission in Tennessee. He tells in his journal of a warning given to him by an angel in a dream, and of the outcome of the experience. This is it:

We arrived that night within five miles of Mr. Akeman's and were kindly entertained by a stranger. During the night I had the following dream: I thought an angel came to us, and told us we were commanded of the Lord to follow a certain straight path, which was pointed out to us, let it lead us wherever it might. After we had walked in it awhile we came to the door of a house, which was in the line of a high wall running north and south, so that we could not go around. I opened the door and saw the room was filled with large serpents, and I shuddered at the sight. My companion said he would not go into the room for fear of the serpents. I told him I would try to go through the room though they killed me, for the Lord commanded it. As I stepped into the room, the serpents coiled themselves up, and raised their heads some two feet from the floor, to spring at me. There was one much larger than the rest, in the center of the room, which raised his head nearly as high as mine and made a spring at me. At that instant I felt as though nothing but the power of God could save me, and I stood still. Just before the serpent reached me he dropped dead at my feet; all the rest dropped dead, swelled up, turned black, burst open, took fire and were consumed before my eyes, and we went through the room unharmed, thanking God for our deliverance.

I awoke in the morning and pondered upon the dream. We took breakfast and started on our journey on Sunday morning to visit Mr. Akeman. I related to my companion my dream, and told him we should see something strange. We had great anticipations in meeting Mr. Akeman, supposing him to be a member of the Church. When we arrived at his house, he received us very coldly, and we soon found that he had apostatized. He brought railing accusations against the Book of Mormon and the authorities of the Church.

Word was sent through all the settlements on the river for twenty miles that two Mormon preachers were in the place. A mob was soon raised, and a warning sent to us to leave immediately or we would be tarred and feathered, ridden on a rail, and hanged. I soon saw who the serpents were. My companion wanted to leave; I told him, no. I would stay and see my dream fulfilled.

There was an old gentleman and lady named Hubbel, who had read the Book of Mormon and believed. Father

Hubbel came to see us, and invited us to make our home with him while we stayed in the place. We did so, and labored for him some three weeks with our axes, clearing land, while we were waiting to see the salvation of God.

February 14th, 1835, was an important day to me. In company with Brother Brown, I took my ax and went into the woods to help Brother Hubbel clear some land. We chopped till 3 o'clock in the afternoon. The spirit of the Lord came upon me like a rushing of mighty wind. The voice of the spirit said, Go up again and visit Mr. Akeman and again bear testimony to him of the truth of the Book of Mormon and of the work of God. I marveled at this and told Brother Brown what the spirit said to me. He replied that I might go if I wished to do so, but that he would not go. I carried my ax to the house and walked up to Mr. Akeman's about one and a half miles through a pleasant grove. While on my way I reflected upon this strange operation of the spirit within me. I was in a deep, gloomy frame of mind and thought. As I approached the house I saw the door open and Mr. Akeman walking the floor. I felt particularly impressed to ask if he was well. He said he never felt better in health. I told him I had come to bear testimony again to him of the truth of the Book of Mormon and of the work of God and of the danger in opposing that work. He was soon filled with wrath and indignation and he opposed me in the strongest terms and raged against the leaders of the Church. My mouth was more closed up than ever before. I felt that the house was filled with devils and with an awful darkness. I felt horrible. I did not understand why the Lord should send me into the midst of such spirits to bear testimony of His work. I felt very strange. My tongue seemed glued to my mouth. I could not speak. I arose to my feet to leave the house. I felt as though the floor moved under my feet and when I stepped upon the ground I felt as though I was sur-rounded by evil spirits. I had a desire to flee as Lot did when he went out of Sodom, without looking behind me. Mr. Akeman followed me out of the door and kept within about four rods of me. Neither of us spoke a word. I knew he was following, but when he was about four rods from the house, the strange feeling left me. When Mr. Akeman reached the place where my feelings so instantly changed, he fell dead at my feet as though he had been struck with a thunderbolt from heaven. I heard him fall to the earth, but I did not look behind me. His daughter stood in the doorway and saw him fall. She fainted and fell at about the same time. Neither of them spoke a word that I could hear. I continued to walk down to Mr. Hubbel's as fast as I could, meditating all the while upon the strange deal' ings of God with me. I still did not know that Mr. Akeman was dead. I arrived at Mr. Hubbel's just at dark in a peculiar state of mind. Supper was ready. We all sat down to the table. The blessing was asked, and I took up my knife and fork and began to eat, when I heard a horse coming up on the full run. I dropped my knife and fork and listened. A man rode up to our door and cried out: 'Mr. Akeman is dead. I want you to go there immediately.' In a moment my eyes were opened, so that I understood the whole matter. I felt satisfied with the dealings of God with me in calling me to go and warn him. (*Life of Wilford Woodruff*, Cowley, pp. 51-53)

When you hold the Aaronic Priesthood you have a right under certain circumstances to be guided by angels. They can come to you direct, or they can show you the way you should go by giving you a dream.

You must be determined, as was President Woodruff, to obey the commandments and to live righteously as a young Latter' day Saint should. If you are worthy, as you come into danger you will be warned. That warning may well come to you by a messenger — an angel. You have the right to receive it, if you live for it.

You may, and should, prepare yourself to defend the Church and its doctrines. And as soon as you can understand them you should prepare yourself to explain the principles to others. Every boy should be like the loyal saints everywhere, able to defend the principles and able to explain them to people not of the faith. The time will soon come when you will be expected to go forth as a missionary.

In the early days young men holding the office of priest actually left home without money, or any means of purchasing food or lodging. They depended upon the Lord to inspire the people to give them food and shelter. They suffered hardships and hunger. They were often wet by the elements — caught in storms with no place to go for shelter. In their desperation they called upon the Lord as their only refuge. The answers to their prayers were often miraculous. Many of these experiences have been handed down in families from generation to generation. Boys today have a feeling that the time for such adventure is past, that the missionaries are not sustained and succored by miraculous events. But all one needs to do is to go out with faith. When the need arises the miracles will take place. Many can testify of words and ideas which have suddenly flooded in on them when they did not know what to say, or how to explain the doctrines effectively. Others have been miraculously fed.

This is the account of one such experience which happened only eleven years ago. It was the joint experience of Elders Truman G. Madsen and Reuel J. Bawden on Prince Edward Island while they were serving as missionaries in the New England Mission:

It was hot and dusty along that country road.

"We're about due for something to eat, don't you think?" said Reuel J. Bawden, pretending he'd had a brilliant new thought.

"Huh!" was all that I could manage in reply.

The thought wasn't a new one. Twenty-four hours had passed since we had eaten anything, and our strength was beginning to wane as we trudged along the sparsely populated backroad. Latter-day Saint missionaries were rather unpopular with these farm folk, I reflected. We'd been forced to sleep in a barn the night before, and now, at 2 o'clock in the afternoon, we had yet to manage something to eat.

Noticing a clump of trees, I said, "Well, let's go tell the Lord about it."

This happened often in our country work . . . going off into the woods to pray. It wasn't a habit — it was a necessity. Who but the Lord could help us in these hostile country areas? We were without purse or scrip. We were on our own. But He in whose work we were engaged was ever within reach, the unfailing resource.

We found a secluded spot, grounded our suitcases with a sigh of relief, and knelt down. Elder B. prayed. It wasn't a long prayer; they seldom were in this work. Forgotten were well-worn phrases and repetitions. We were praying for urgent needs. It didn't take long to express them.

"Father, wilt thou open the way for us to have a bite to eat."

My "Amen" was heartfelt.

As we stood and donned our hats, I noticed a ripple in the small brooklet that gurgled through the grove. A trout rose to strike at a fly. I smiled.

"Oh, for a fishing pole!" I said, half aloud.

"What's wrong with what you have in your hand?" said Elder B.

I looked down at the tattered umbrella and chuckled.

Elder B. wasn't smiling.

"Hmmm," he said, "you've got thread; I've got a safety pin; and we ought to be able to find a worm around and —"

"And you've got a few matches in your grip," I finished for him. "What are we waiting for?"

A handy man was Elder B. In a few minutes he had doubled and redoubled enough thread to make a line. Then with his nail clipper he fashioned a hook from his safety pin, and I sharpened it with a fingernail file. I found a worm under a stump, and tying the line to the umbrella, crept up to the stream.

This was a pretty far-fetched situation, I thought to myself — fishing with makeshift gear — and fishing in dead earnest, not for sport. I recalled one of my father's statements, "Always at hand is the thing needed, if you only have the wit and wisdom to recognize it." Was this wit and wisdom, I asked myself, or inspiration?

I dangled the line over the grassy bank and floated it downstream.

Can this be the way the Lord is going to answer our prayer, I thought, or do I just have a flair for the unusual? Well, we're his servants. We're promised that the way will be opened. The Lord had answered us before. Now why can't he arrange to have that fish bite? He's brought us this far, and —

WHAM!

I pulled, fast! The trout sailed over my head, off the hook, and onto the bank.

"Man!" I chortled, "Mr. Fish musta been pretty hungry too."

Elder B. was laughing. But there were tears in his eyes. I stared incredulously, first at the umbrella, then at the fish. Elder B. broke the spell.

"Find another worm," he said. "There must be more fish in that brook."

Worms there were, and trout too. They hit that line as if they hadn't seen a fly or worm in weeks. It didn't take me long to catch five more. It was too good to be true. In a few short minutes six trout were broiling over a small fire.

We didn't eat those fish without blessing them. And when we said, "Father in heaven, we thank thee for this food," it came from the heart. We ate them, relished them, fins and all. We were warm inside when we finished — warm from the fish, warm from deep-rooted gratitude.

We picked up our suitcases and began trudging down the narrow road.

"You know," said Elder B., as we walked with re-newed strength, "the Lord is a mighty generous employer!" (*Improvement Era,* Vol. 51, p. 151, March, 1948.)

You can have the satisfying experience of convincing some-one of the truth of the gospel you are trying to live. You do this by the testimony within you, but your appeal is made through the senses. The person listening must sense somehow your ab-solute sincerity; your personal life must advertise that you use its principles as your law of conduct; you must have in your mind knowledge of the principles which you have gained by study, thinking, and discussions with your teachers.

You now have a right to do all this: The cottage meetings you attend, your speeches in Sacrament meetings, your two and one-half minute talks — these are your beginnings. Take ad-vantage of them.

Third Key — BAPTISM BY IMMERSION FOR THE REMISSION OF SINS

When you are a priest you will be invited by the bishop to baptize some of the children of your ward. This is a happy experience, and one which will prepare you for like experiences in the mission field. There you will have one of your supreme joys. It is a pleasure to baptize a person who has repented of his sins and accepted the gospel principles, but it is a joy to perform the ordinance of baptism on a person who has learned from you these principles. While they are not truly your converts — for they get the witness from the Holy Ghost — yet you found them; you caught their interest; you explained the doctrine with the assistance of the power of the Holy Ghost within you. And the joy of baptizing one of these cannot be bought. It can be had only by obeying the law and seeking out the honest in heart. No boys of any church on earth, except yours, can look forward to the use of this great key which has been given to you. And you will get the same joy if you convert your neighboring friend at home or at school. Some of our finest converts were made members by the work of our young men in the army and in college. And some families have had joy in converting their next-door neighbors. Be prepared for it when your opportunity comes to you.

And don't forget that the keys to these three great possibilities are held by the President of the Church. He turns these keys in your behalf through the bishopric of your ward. Stay close to the bishop.

CHAPTER 16

THE PROPHET'S WORDS ARE FINAL

We have been considering what John the Baptist gave to the Prophet Joseph Smith and to Oliver Cowdery on that fateful day in May, 1829. From that great event we should draw one more important lesson, and that is that so far as we are con' cerned, the words of the Prophet are final. We don't take anybody's word against his.

Several years after the coming of John, Oliver Cowdery wrote a letter to a friend in which he described the ecstasy with which he took part in the restoration of the Aaronic Priesthood. In that letter he quoted John the Baptist. As one would expect from an un'memorized event, Oliver didn't quote in the same words and with quite the same meaning that Joseph Smith recorded in the Thirteenth Section of the Doctrine and Covenants.

This is what he wrote: "But dear Brother, think, further think for a moment, what joy filled our hearts, and with what surprise we must have bowed, (for who would not have bowed the knee for such a blessing?) when we received under his hand the Holy Priesthood as he said, 'Upon you my fellow servants, in the name of Messiah, I confer this Priesthood and this authority, which shall remain upon the earth, that the sons of Levi may yet offer an offering unto the Lord in righteousness!' "

Now here are the words of the 13th Section of the Doctrine and Covenants:

> Upon you my fellow servants, in the name of Messiah I confer the Priesthood of Aaron, which holds the keys of the ministering of angels, and of the gospel of repentance, and of baptism by immersion for the remission of sins; and this shall never be taken again from the earth, until the sons of Levi do offer again an offering unto the Lord in righteousness.

You will promptly see some differences. I have heard a man of some prominence say, referring to the sons of Levi offering an offering, that he likes Brother Cowdery's words better, for they had a clearer meaning to him. But whatever they meant to him he was laboring under the wrong principle. There can be only one mouthpiece for the Lord or for messengers sent from the Lord. No two people can, from memory, describe an event exactly alike. The statements of both have chances for error. But in this case the Prophet held the keys to declare, and by the use of those keys his statement will be taken.

You as holders of the Aaronic Priesthood will be tempted many times to believe an account of an event, an experience, or a quotation, which seems to differ or does differ from the account of the Prophet who was the chief recipient. Never make the mistake of putting the words of the assistant ahead of the words of the Prophet. This course will keep you steady and safe. Men and boys make mistakes. The Prophet stated he was not infallible. But his word will stand against others when the others differ with him.

CHAPTER 17

YOUR AUTHORITY -- ONLY FOR THOSE BOYS WHO WANT TO KNOW

There comes a time in the life of every young man when just to be told by a teacher is not enough. He needs to see for himself, to ponder the truth, to acquire depth of soul. So he needs to turn to the written word of revelation. This short chapter calls your attention to some revelations which you should want to know more about. It will also test your ability to listen to the whisperings of the spirit of truth. As you read them you should have a feeling steal over you concerning their truth. Then, too, you should be impressed with their importance. Joseph Smith received here the foundation knowledge of the history of the Priesthood. How it was preserved in the earliest human times is described here, as well as its importance to you. Read and learn.

Of course, there will be some who will not want to read. Those boys can just skip the remainder of the chapter. So let's begin:

> And the sons of Moses, according to the Holy Priesthood which he received under the hand of his father-in-law, Jethro;
>
> And Jethro received it under the hand of Caleb;
>
> And Caleb received it under the hand of Elihu;
>
> And Elihu under the hand of Jeremy;
>
> And Jeremy under the hand of Gad;
>
> And Gad under the hand of Esaias;
>
> And Esaias received it under the hand of God.
>
> Esaias also lived in the days of Abraham, and was blessed of him —

Which Abraham received the priesthood from Melchizedek, who received it through the lineage of his fathers, even till Noah;

And from Noah till Enoch, through the lineage of their fathers;

And from Enoch to Abel, who was slain by the conspiracy of his brother, who received the priesthood by the commandments of God, by the hand of his father Adam, who was the first man —

Which priesthood continueth in the church of God in all genera' tions, and is without beginning of days or end of years.

And the Lord confirmed the priesthood also upon Aaron and his seed, throughout all their generations, which priesthood also continueth and abideth forever with the priesthood which is after the holiest order of God.

And this greater priesthood administereth the gospel and holdeth the key of the mysteries of the kingdom, even the key of knowledge of God.

Therefore, in the ordinances thereof, the power of godliness is manifest.

And without the ordinances thereof, and the authority of the priesthood, the power of godliness is not manifest unto men in the flesh;

For without this no man can see the face of God, even the Father, and live.

Now this Moses plainly taught to the children of Israel in the wilderness, and sought diligently to sanctify his people that they might behold the face of God;

But they hardened their hearts and could not endure his presence; therefore, the Lord in his wrath, for his anger was kindled against them, swore that they should not enter into his rest while in the wilderness, which rest is the fulness of his glory.

Therefore, he took Moses out of their midst, and the Holy Priesthood also;

And the lesser priesthood continued, which priesthood holdeth the key of the ministering of angels and the preparatory gospel; (Doc. & Cov. 84:6-26)

If you read completely through this quotation you will see that the Priesthood was conferred by descent from Adam to Moses, and that Moses held it. The line of authority passed through Melchizedek and Abraham.

You already know that finally Moses was taken and that Aaron and the Lesser Priesthood were left to administer in earthly things. You will understand better if you know that the offices in the Priesthood are appendages to the Priesthood.

And again, the offices of elder and bishop are necessary append' ages belonging unto the high priesthood. (Doc. & Cov. 84:29)

And you will also see that this applies to the Aaronic Priest' hood offices, too:

And again, the offices of teacher and deacon are necessary ap' pendages belonging to the lesser priesthood, which priesthood was con' firmed upon Aaron and his sons. (Doc. & Cov. 84:30)

This applies as well to all the offices in the Church, for they are appendages to the Priesthood after the Order of the Son of God.

All other authorities or offices in the church are appendages to this priesthood.

But there are two divisions or grand heads — one is the Mel' chizedek Priesthood, and the other is the Aaronic or Levitical Priest' hood. (Doc. & Cov. 107:5-6)

In the future the sons of Moses and of Aaron are to offer an acceptable offering to the Lord in his Holy House, in righteousness. We do not have the deatils of this great event, but we do know one thing: we may become the Sons of Moses and of Aaron for a starter:

For whoso is faithful unto the obtaining these two priesthoods of which I have spoken, and the magnifying their calling, are sancti' fied by the Spirit unto the renewing of their bodies.

They become the sons of Moses and of Aaron and the seed of Abraham, and the church and kingdom, and the elect of God. (Doc. & Cov. 84:33-34)

Belonging to the House of Israel is a serious business. It is a vast, far'reaching relationship based on the ties of the Priest' hood reaching clear back to Adam, with special blessings on those who are of Israel — or of Abraham — and who will accept by adoption the Priesthood to become the sons of Moses, of Aaron, of Abraham, and of the Church of the First Born — which is Christ's.

Verse 39 of the 84th Section says that those who accept this Priesthood receive the oath and the covenant which belong to the Priesthood:

61

Therefore, all those who receive the priesthood, receive this oath and covenant of my Father, which he cannot break, neither can it be moved.

But whoso breaketh this covenant after he hath received it, and altogether turneth therefrom, shall not have forgiveness of sins in this world nor in the world to come. (Doc. & Cov. 84:40-41)

So you will make a covenant some time and this will bind you to the Lord Jesus Christ unless you break it. This is from the *Doctrine and Covenants Commentary* on Section 84:

Oath and covenant — These two terms stand for the arrangement between God and man regarding the plan of salvation. The covenant is, in the Scriptures, sometimes called God's "counsel," and sometimes His "oath," and His "promise" (Comp. Ps. 89:3, 4, 105:8, 11; Heb. 6:13-20; Luke 1:68-75; Gal. 3:15-18). All these terms mean His "covenant."

Here in these verses (33-41) we learn that the Lord has promised to all those who are faithful, and who magnify their calling, that they shall be in fellowship with both the Father and the Son, and if they continue faithful, they shall eventually inherit "all that my Father hath." This means that they shall become the sons of God, joint heirs with Jesus Christ, and as expressed in Section 76:55-60, they shall receive the fulness of his glory. When the Lord offers the fulness of his glory on conditions of faithfulness, he attaches a penalty for the breaking of such a glorious and far-reaching covenant. Therefore he has decreed that all those who trample this covenant (which every person receiving the Melchizedek Priesthood receives) under his feet, "and altogether turneth therefrom, shall not have forgiveness of sins in this world nor in the world to come." This means that all who treat this covenant of the Priesthood with contempt shall never have the privilege of exercising it in the world to come. Therefore they will be barred from celestial exaltation.

You can well afford to live worthy to enter into the covenant. The Aaronic Priesthood will help you gain this great boon.

CHAPTER 18 •

"WHEN THEY SAW YOUR CONDUCT -- !"

Every boy who holds the Priesthood advertises that he is on his way to become a son of God our Father. Since no boy is a hypocrite nor wants to sail under false colors, he will do all he can to live up to what the Lord expects of him. His efforts can be expressed in two general ways.

1. How he conducts his personal life; what he considers to be the ideal of his conduct, and

2. How he responds to meetings called by the bishop and how well he does the labors assigned to him.

You have a fairly clear path on No. 2. The meetings are provided. You go. So do all the other boys. You are assigned to do a job. Usually you do it. The other boys do the same. You are part of an easily understood pattern of conduct. While nothing much happens to you at the moment if you don't do as you are expected, usually you have little trouble in being on hand to take part in the ordinary functions of the ward.

But your personal life is different. No one can know just what you are thinking. You are the only one who knows the thoughts which are yours when you are alone in the hills, or in a movie, or at a football game, or at a dance. You might say to yourself, "I hold the Priesthood — how do my thoughts measure up, right now?" Then you might add, "And are my acts following my thoughts?"

It will be a long time before you finally become, inside, what your thoughts lead you to be. But it will be a very short time until the people around you are influenced by what you do each day.

When I was a boy I formed a very great prejudice against a prominent church — not ours. I thought it was bad, that it was worse than bad, that it was entirely evil. When I saw people that I knew go into the chapel of that church I thought they were evil, too, and I kept as far away from them as I could. I just didn't like them. Do you know why I felt that way? It was because of Pete Simpson. Pete was a bully. He was big, he was strong, he was tough — and advertised the fact. He smoked cigarettes. (When I was a boy a cigarette smoker was thought to be the most daring of all the evildoers. Times change.) He played hookey from school. And he made my life miserable by chasing me constantly with a threat to lick me if he caught me. He never caught me, because while he was larger than I, he couldn't run as fast. But he belonged to *that* church. I formed the idea that belonging to that church was the main reason why he was so bad. So I formed an early opinion of the church and its people, based upon the acts of one boy. I know now that this particular boy was not a good member. Probably he didn't ever attend meetings — but he belonged. To this day if you should mention the name of his church my feelings of dislike come back. Occasionally I pass its chapel. My dislike flares up in spite of myself. Of course I know better, and I now conquer the feeling — but it persists — and persists. We cannot easily shake the feelings and prejudices formed while we are young.

Alma was the leader of the Church in his day. He had several sons. They were different, one from another, but one, Corianton, really got busy in doing evil and acting the way he shouldn't. He had his own life to live, and if he wanted to wreck it, who should interfere? He didn't seem to realize that no one can do anything without influencing others.

Alma called his son in and talked to him. I have never read his words without being filled with the desire to have all boys who hold the Priesthood remember the words whenever they get into a questionable position.

64

Picture a rebellious son who was bringing his father, who was President of the Church in that day, into disrepute because the son wouldn't obey.

He said to Corianton:

> . . . Behold, O my son, how great iniquity ye brought upon the Zoramites; for *when they saw your conduct they would not believe in my words.* (Alma 39:11)

The anxiety of a righteous man to bring the gospel to people who are not members and his effort to convince people of the truth is sometimes made ineffective by the acts of men and boys who belong to the Church, for they are watched by these people. They will judge our pure and holy principles by the way these principles influence us.

Priesthood holders must learn to live so that when people hear of the gospel they will be bound to say, "It must be wonderful. Those boys in the neighborhood are the finest boys we know."

CHAPTER 19 •

WORD OF WISDOM

After you have been given the privilege of holding the Priesthood, a great change begins in your life. This change has very simple beginnings and may stay simple and easy to understand, or it can get complicated. This is it: Now you begin to be on your own. You will, more and more, make decisions, while your mother and father will begin to make them less and less for you. This is part of the process of becoming a man. Perhaps we can help you to see more clearly the issues and point out to you the facts concerning your course of action. Let's keep it simple, and keep ourselves from getting complicated.

A very simple definition was given to John the Beloved:

> Whosoever committeth sin transgresseth also the law; for sin is the transgression of the law. (1st John 3:4)

So let's find the laws by which we are expected to make our way into manhood. Once we know the law we can keep from breaking it.

THE WORD OF WISDOM

Your greatest temptation as a boy will be to break this law. Other boys will try to persuade you to do it. Evil men desiring to sell their enslaving products will publicly advertise them in a most alluring and enticing manner. The nearer you grow to manhood the greater the pressure will be to break this commandment. Now is the time to form your habits in conformity with it.

The "Word of Wisdom" is the 89th Section of the Doctrine and Covenants. No more, no less. There are other words of wisdom, of course, and we shall talk about some of them, but when we say, "Keep the Word of Wisdom," we mean the 89th Section. What does it give as wisdom? It warns you against the conspiracies of evil men in the last days:

> Behold, verily, thus saith the Lord unto you: In consequence of evils and designs which do and will exist in the hearts of conspiring men in the last days, I have warned you, and forewarn you, by giving you this word of wisdom . . . (verse 4)

There was no widespread conspiracy to enslave men through habitforming drugs into using a particular product when this was said, but since then men have deliberately thought out methods to accomplish this very thing. You see the advertisements for their products on all sides — not seeking older people but pointing to young folk. Let's see if we can discover what the Lord meant, in part at least.

> . . . inasmuch as any man drinketh wine or strong drink among you, behold it is not good . . . (verse 5)

Open any magazine. Recently there has been running a series of pictures of happy family life with the caption, "Beer belongs — enjoy it." Lately they say "Beer belongs — to the fun of living." This series implies that unless the family has beer on the table, they are missing true enjoyment. This, of course, is not true, as you well know. Then there has been another series called "Men of distinction." In these advertisements one is given the idea that men of great ability drink the whiskey advertised by this company. They imply that a man isn't distinguished unless he drinks not only whiskey but the special brand of this company. You will learn by reading the more recent advertisements that the people of the world who are really smart and intelligent don't settle for anything less than vodka.

The men who advertise these products are "conspiring men."

What are the facts? Beer, wine, brandy, whiskey, vodka contain alcohol in varying amounts. Alcohol is a harmful depressant which, when taken in any quantity, has an effect on the nervous controls of the body. The more the quantity that is drunk, the greater the effect. Especially, it distorts judgments. The drinker *thinks* he has control, and is loud in proclaiming it, but he doesn't have it.

Here is an experiment for you. Take the family newspaper. List the automobile accidents which appear during any one week. Put an X by those in which drinking was listed as a possible cause. If you want to investigate further you can go to the police station and talk to the officers about any accident. Here you will discover that many involve those who have been drinking, but that the newspaper doesn't mention the fact.

Accidents are only one phase of it. The breaking up of homes, divorce and its terrible effects on children, often are caused by drinking. Most serious crimes have their foundation in drink. If you are alert you will notice that your chances of gaining any good from the practice of drinking are at about zero percentage. So the Lord says:

"It is not good, neither meet in the sight of your Father . . ." (verse 5) Are you curious about it? Here is one thing you'd better never discover: how it feels to drink. There are some things one doesn't do to satisfy curiosity — one doesn't look down the barrel of a gun and then pull the trigger to see if he can be fast enough to dodge the bullet. Liquor is a loaded gun and no one was ever fast enough to dodge its effects.

CHAPTER 20 •

WORD OF WISDOM
(Continued)

And again, tobacco is not for the body, neither for the belly, and is not good for man, but is an herb for bruises and for all sick cattle, to be used with judgment and skill. (verse 8)

One never sees an advertisement telling him how to use tobacco for bruises, or for sick animals. We all use its poisons to kill insects on roses and fruit trees, but apparently no one has capitalized on the hint given by the Lord for its use in helping suffering animals. He said, "It is not good for man."

I ride trains and airplanes a great deal in traveling about for the Church. It is extremely difficult to escape the fumes of countless cigarettes in crowded trains or cabins of planes. The people who smoke have no consideration for people who do not. The air gets thick with the fumes as smokers exhale, often blowing the smoke into my face. If I lie in a Pullman berth or a motel bed at night, the blankets and pillow are saturated with the stale odor, which becomes worse with age. About the worst case of halitosis you can find is the breath of a person who smokes.

Yet here is one product for which conspiring men have gone the whole distance of lies and misrepresentations to persuade you to indulge. The tobacco industry deliberately started out a campaign to get women to smoke. It took about two years of pictured advertisements beginning with a happy expression just to be near men smokers. The next step was to show the girl holding the cigarette in her hand, and finally between her lips. Then of course it was fairly simple to show how a romance between a young man and young woman couldn't possibly be complete nor happy unless the couple were constantly smoking.

It's about this silly:

Boy: "Will you marry me? I love you."

Girl: "Yes, I love you too."

Boy: "Have a cigarette."

Girl: "Sure — "

Boy: "Now kiss me." (They kiss, amid curling smoke). Implied: They live happily ever after, soothed and contented with Whozits cigarettes.

Once a person smokes he is not very happy unless others join him. Notice how uneasy a smoker is when he finds himself the only one in the crowd. I saw a fellow once who passed a pack of cigarettes around, offering them to each of six other men. None were smokers, so they declined politely. He lit a cigarette, took two or three puffs, and threw it away. He couldn't stand the unspoken rudeness with which he forced those men to endure his smoke.

But let there be even one other smoker in a crowd and, reinforced by this one other, he now will forget all courtesy and, regardless of comfort or consideration, will impose his fumes on the non-smokers. He will become brazen about it, as though he is saying, "I have a right to do this and you can't stop me, so don't try."

I do not need to point out the cost of smoking. It can easily amount to $7.50 per month per person, which is $90.00 per year. This will be a minimum as soon as the habit is formed, based on about one pack per day.

Nor do I need to convince anyone of intelligence that it is physically bad for a person. The doctors of England and America are not joking when they say that your chances for serious disease are greater if you smoke. It is true that lung cancer is much more prevalent among smokers than among non-smokers. It is true that heart disease — as well as heart failure — is greater among smokers. It is true that not a college or high school coach in America who knows his business will allow smokers to play on his teams. No athlete worth his salt will smoke, and no athlete with any sense of honor will let his name be used in advertising cigarettes.

In spite of all of this, probably your first temptation to violate the law of the Lord will be by cigarettes. Other boys do smoke, and as you meet them they will offer them to you. If you refuse they will mock you and imply that you are a sissy, a mama's boy. They will make you feel that you can't be a man unless you flout your folks and get on their standard of conduct. There is only one way to meet this temptation. When they try to persuade you, stand firm. Say "No." Don't even say "thanks." Look them straight in the eye and say, "I don't smoke" — then do your best to run around with a crowd of boys who don't smoke. If you go with boys who smoke, the chances are good that sooner or later you will smoke, too. There is an old poem by Alexander Pope which will apply here:

> Vice is a monster of such frightful mien,
> As to be hated, needs but to be seen;
> Yet seen too oft, familiar with her face,
> We first endure, then pity, then embrace.
> (from *Essay on Man* by Alexander Pope)

Watch out! You are forewarned by the Lord. Are you forearmed to resist?

CHAPTER 21

WORD OF WISDOM
(Continued)

"And again hot drinks are not for the body or belly." (verse 9) This is a very plain statement, and it was plain in the days of Joseph Smith. People argued then about it, even as they do now. No one doubts that any liquid, boiling hot, would do damage to the membranous walls of the esophagus and stomach. No one doubts that coffee or tea brewed at boiling temperature and then cooled with ice until well chilled is not at the moment a hot drink in the sense of applied heat. Some people are quite smug about drinking iced tea in the summer, saying that it is not a hot drink. Do you think they have a reasonable interpretation?

Today we have good reason to know that milk, water, lemonade, and orangeade could be heated and drunk without harmful effects. They are still what they are. And we know that coffee and tea contain stimulants, whether they are hot or cold.

Now what is a stimulant? It is a spur, a whip. Its action is to force muscles which it affects to move faster. It does not feed the muscles; it just pushes them to more work. And for a short time in emergencies this could be necessary. But in the long run to spur or whip them constantly to action without giving them the necessary fuel to make them go eventually tires the muscles more than if they had gone their regular pace. It helps us to go faster for a few moments, but the stimulated body can't keep up the faster pace.

If you are strong and have good endurance and know you have the strength to climb a mountain in six hours, say, and then if you find that by drinking a cup of coffee you can climb the mountain in five hours, you would have gained an hour — but you would be much more tired when the effects of the stimulant wore off. If you had to climb the same mountain again the next day, you could still do it easily in your six hours. And a third and fourth day. But if you tried to do it in five hours with your stimulant it wouldn't be quite so easy, and about the fourth day you'd be so tired you'd have to take a day off and rest. Stimulants make things easier at the moment but collect their toll in the end. Too, they have the disadvantage of being habit forming. After a while one finds himself craving them, not able to get along, even normally, without them.

I have seen the effects of coffee on soldiers. I was a soldier in the first World War. Every morning the men who drank coffee regularly had a hard time getting started. They were grouchy, irritable, crabbing over their conditions. Finally they would be called to mess (breakfast). They would drink two or three cups of bitter, black coffee. Ah, now they felt better, and for a time the world was rosy. I used to test myself. I drank only water. Before breakfast I felt good. After breakfast I felt the same. There was no difference. Morning after morning it was the same. I had the strength before that I had after. If by any chance my buddies had to wait until noon for their coffee there was no living with them, so irritable were they. I saw enough of it to know that a whip is no good. I had the same experience with cowboys on the range.

Where did we get the idea that "hot drinks" referred to tea and coffee? Here is an account of what was said at a meeting held in Nauvoo on the last Sunday in May, 1842. The *Times and Seasons* reported it as follows:

> And again "hot drinks are not for the body, or belly"; there are many who wonder what this can mean; whether it refers to tea, or coffee, or not. I say it does refer to tea, and coffee. Why is it that we are frequently dull and languid? It is because we break the word of wisdom, disease preys upon our system, our understandings are darkened, and we do not comprehend the things of God; the devil takes advantage of us, and we fall into temptation. (*Times and Seasons,* Smith, Hyrum, June 1, 1842, Vol. III, No. 15, p. 800)

Hyrum Smith, the Patriarch and counselor to the Prophet, made the talk; Joseph Smith sat on the stand. If he hadn't approved he'd have said so. That makes it official for tea and coffee.

Later Brigham Young at a conference of the Church presented the subject:

> President Young rose to put the motion and called on all the sisters who will leave off the use of tea, coffee, etc., to manifest it by raising the right hand; seconded and carried.

> And then put the following motion; calling on all the boys who were under ninety years of age who would covenant to leave off the use of tobacco, whisky, and all things mentioned in the Word of Wisdom, to manifest it in the same manner, which was carried unanimously.

President Young amongst other things said he knew the goodness of the people, and the Lord bears with our weakness; we must serve the Lord, and those who go with me will keep the Word of Wisdom, and if the High Priests, Seventies, the Elders, and others will not serve the Lord, we will sever them from the Church. I will draw the line and know who is for the Lord and who is not, and those who will not keep the Word of Wisdom, I will cut off from the Church; I throw out a challenge to all men and women. (Tuesday, September 9, 1851 — General Conference)

That should make the stand of the Church plan enough.

NOT THE WORD OF WISDOM—
BUT GOOD PLAIN COMMON SENSE

One more thing: if you drink coffee because of the stimulant in it, and chemists discover that caffeine is the stimulating and habit-forming drug in coffee, would you be justified in drinking any drink which contained caffeine, even though it was not called coffee? Another question. Why do they put caffeine in soft drinks? Certainly not to stimulate you. But if they can get you to form a *habit* of drinking their drink, and by adding caffeine create in you a feeling that you want it, then they can sell more, and make more money. That is the fundamental idea behind the "cola" drinks. There are a large number of them.

If any food or drink crosses a state line the container must be labeled as to its contents. Here is the label from a can of Shasta Cola made in San Francisco, California, and Seattle, Washington: "Ingredients: Carbonated water, sugar, caramel color, cola nut extractive, citrus oils and other flavors, phosphoric acid, and *caffeine,* U.S.P."

Here is a project. Go to any drugstore which sells Coca-Cola at its soda fountain by the glass. Ask the druggist for an empty can in which the syrup was shipped into your state. He usually has one or two empty cans or bottles. Read the label. You can do the same thing for any of the cola drinks, and for a few not labeled "cola."

74

But you won't find the label on a bottle you get from a dispensing machine. The reason for that is that the syrup crossing the state line is labeled, but the bottles are filled and sold within the state and usually do not have to be labeled — as long as they aren't shipped across the state lines.

Now you do not need to ask anyone about whether or not to drink cola drinks. They are not specified in the Word of Wisdom, but they contain the same ingredient which makes coffee objectionable.

What do you think? Will you need a special commandment from the Lord or can you make your own decision on what to do about them?

CHAPTER 22 •

WORD OF WISDOM
(Continued)

And again, verily I say unto you, all wholesome herbs God hath ordained for the constitution, nature, and use of man —

Every herb in the season thereof, and every fruit in the season thereof; all these to be used with prudence and thanksgiving. (verses 10-11)

Vegetables are herbs. So are tomatoes. Don't you think that the Lord was wise when he said that we could eat all *wholesome* herbs? He didn't try to say just how to prepare them for eating. But we can cook them all, although some are good raw. We can peel them, or eat the skins. We can bake them, boil them, broil them, fry them. There is no restriction and no special way to cook them which is better than another. The same is true of fruit. The only reason you should not eat any of these is that one or another might disagree. I know a woman who breaks out with hives every time she eats strawberries. She shouldn't eat strawberries. But generally all are edible, all are available, and all can be eaten in the season in which they grow; or they can be preserved, canned, or frozen to be eaten later. I'm glad we have cold storage. Apples, as well as many other fruits and vegetables, can be had in February. Our modern diet would be very uninteresting along about March if we lived as our grandparents had to. The freezer has made eating a pleasure the year round.

> Yea, flesh also of beasts and of the fowls of the air, I, the Lord, have ordained for the use of man with thanksgiving; nevertheless they are to be used sparingly;

> And it is pleasing unto me that they should not be used, only in times of winter, or of cold, or famine. (verses 12-13)

If you have read this closely you will readily see that the Lord allows you to eat meat and fowl. His only restrictive suggestion is that it will please him if you eat it sparingly, and then in times of hunger, famine, or cold. Anciently the children of Israel were forbidden to eat the meat of any cloven-hoofed animal which didn't chew the cud. That made pork a forbidden food, for its hoofs are cloven and it doesn't chew the cud. Some people like to assume that the law of ancient Israel in this respect still applies, but this statement in the Word of Wisdom takes precedence over the ancient law. There was good reason, we can see now, behind the restriction anciently. Pigs are scavengers by nature. Given sufficient hunger they will eat anything — good or bad. In those days pigs did considerable roaming around, picking up offal as well as what little vegetation they could. So the meat could be on the unpalatable side. But worse, there is a disease called trichinosis which is really an infection. It makes a person quite sick. The trichinae are present in the flesh of pork. If the pork is insufficiently cooked — underdone — a person eating it can be infected. In those days, cooking methods being often very poor, it was easy to get trichinosis.

It still is. Suppose that you go out on a cookout, or an overnight hike. For your meat you take a pork chop. (Often pork is cheaper than hamburger, and your folks have to watch the budget.) You start to cook your supper, and you fry your

76

chop. But the fire isn't very good, and you are in a hurry, being very hungry, so the meat isn't cooked quite enough. In your hunger it tastes done, but it isn't quite cooked, so that the trichinae are not killed. You could become infected, and be in for a miserable time.

Today we know about the germs in pork flesh. We see to it that when it is cooked it is a thorough job. Then, too, pigs which go to our market are well fed on good clean grain and other products designed to bring them to prime condition for top prices. Times are different, and so is the law. What I have just said is my idea of it. This is my reasoning as to why the Lord restricted Israel anciently and doesn't restrict us today. Remember, too, that this is a law of the earth — eating earthly things. It is given to us to help keep healthy while we are here.

> All grain is ordained for the use of man and of beasts, to be the staff of life, not only for man but for the beasts of the field, and the fowls of heaven, and all wild animals that run or creep on the earth; . . .
>
> All grain is good for the food of man; as also the fruit of the vine; that which yieldeth fruit, whether in the ground or above the ground —
>
> Nevertheless, wheat for man, and corn for the ox, and oats for the horse, and rye for the fowls and for swine, and for all beasts of the field, and barley for all useful animals, and for mild drinks, as also other grain. (verses 14, 16, 17)

Now you will notice that you can eat any grain, but that wheat takes top listing; that any animal may eat any grain, although they do better on a specified kind. You don't know much about horses nowadays, but when horses were the source of travel, oats were fed, chiefly. And perhaps once rye was the chief food of hogs, but today in the middlewest corn has proved an excellent fattener and conditioner.

So you have great freedom in the choice of food. The Word of Wisdom is wise counsel given by the Lord for the good of man. Summed up in a sentence, the Lord says: You may eat anything, but don't be foolish enough to partake of plants which contain habit-forming drugs, or of fermented drinks which contain alcohol.

Some folk argue that when they eat too much they are breaking the Word of Wisdom. But this is not so. Certainly they are not wise. But except in the case of meat the amounts you eat are not specified. Even in the case of meat it is a matter of how often, not how much. The matter of quantity is something that must be determined by conditions. When I was seventeen, growing fast, maturing, I worked on a farm pitching hay. The work began at five a.m. with the chores, then breakfast, and to the field at seven a.m. Work until noon — five hours; one hour dinner time; work from one till six — five hours; supper; chores until eight. That made a day lasting about thirteen hours, of which ten hours was hard, steady, back-breaking work. I marvel at the amount of food I ate while I was working at that job — so did the man who owned the farm. I don't believe he made any money on me. I just couldn't get enough.

Now I arise at five a.m., do a little gardening, cut the lawn, shovel a little snow in the winter. If I ate one-eighth as much I'd be sick. It is not wise for me now to eat what I could when I was a growing boy, but it is not a part of the Word of Wisdom.

CHAPTER 23

WORD OF WISDOM
(Concluded)

And all saints who remember to keep and do these sayings, *walking in obedience to the commandments,* shall receive health in their navel and marrow to their bones;

And shall find wisdom and great treasures of knowledge, even hidden treasures;

And shall run and not be weary, and shall walk and not faint.

And I, the Lord, give unto them a promise, that the destroying angel shall pass by them, as the children of Israel, and not slay them. Amen. (D. & C. 89:18-21)

This is a promise made by the Lord. If you do your part, he will do as he says. But please notice that the words in italics form a statement that many people ignore when they think they are in harmony with and keeping the Word of Wisdom. This is it:

". . . walking in obedience to the commandments, . . ."

That is the catch. You cannot hope for wealth and strength merely by controlling what you eat, but you must keep all the commandments to receive the blessing. Eating is just the physical phase of it.

OTHER WISDOM NOT IN SECTION 89

What are some of these other commandments? We know about tithing and fasting to help the poor with an offering. We know about going to the ward Sacrament meetings, and helping. Here are a few which are very important and which must be kept if you expect to receive the blessing promised in the Word of Wisdom:

Therefore, cease from all your light speeches, from all laughter, from all your lustful desires, from all your pride and light-mindedness, and from all your wicked doings. . . .

See that ye love one another; cease to be covetous; learn to impart one to another as the gospel requires.

Cease to be idle; cease to be unclean; cease to find fault one with another; cease to sleep longer than is needful; retire to thy bed early, that ye may not be weary; arise early, that your bodies and your minds may be invigorated.

And above all things, clothe yourselves with the bond of charity, as with a mantle, which is the bond of perfectness and peace.

Pray always, that ye may not faint, until I come. Behold, and lo, I will come quickly, and receive you unto myself. Amen. (Doc. & Cov. 88:121, 123-126)

And there are others which you learn as you progress.

From these short admonitions, you can see that the Lord wants you and me to become well-adjusted people — not faddists, but holy men, practicing the virtues which make us finally what we are intended to be. One would not expect a boy who didn't know the revelations to know why we keep the commandments, but we are holders of the Priesthood — representing the Lord on earth and preparing to make a covenant with the Lord that we will keep all of his commandments, that he in his turn will take us back into his presence and give us his glory and eternal life. That gives us purpose. Be thankful that we have purpose in our acts.

CHAPTER 24 •

CHASTITY

We were meeting in the Seventies' Room of the Salt Lake Temple and were discussing the far-reaching effects resulting from disobedience. The particular point of discussion centered upon disobedience to instruction given us by the President of the Church. President Antoine R. Ivins spoke up and said that our talk reminded him of an experience he had. He said that a young woman had reported to him for a missionary interview. In the course of the conversation she confessed that her conduct on one occasion had not been what it should be, but that she had repented of it and had since proved her repentance by living as she should. After hearing her, President Ivins said that he would forgive her, the church would forgive her, and as he understood it, the repentant sinner could receive forgiveness from the Lord, if the repentant one lived the laws of God the remainder of her life. The young woman replied, "The Lord can, perhaps will, forgive me, you will forgive me, the Church will forgive, *but I cannot forgive myself.*" That is about the sum of the matter of committing sin. The person at some time is brought up short with a sharp conscience, and then as long as he lives he wishes he had resisted and had not committed the act.

This remorse can be as sharp as a two-edged sword. It has driven many people to despair. Were it not for the gift of repentance granted us by Christ the Lord those who are in this situation would lose hope entirely.

The Eternal Father is all-wise. Being our father he knows the means by which we can come into his presence. We have been taught through revelation that the highest purpose we can have in this life is to become sealed to a young woman and then, cherishing her, together raise righteous children. Only on that basis can we finally achieve our highest goal — eternal life. He has said that without marriage a man or woman cannot enter into his presence. We are fortunate today that we have temples and the proper authority restored so that we can be sealed.

In addition to this law given us it appears that the Father wants us to experience, in part, what it means to create. He has allowed us the privilege of organizing the physical bodies of his children, and of then nurturing them into righteousness. So sacred is this trust that its abuse is considered one of the most serious of sins. Every boy who is a candidate for celestial glory (and every holder of the Priesthood is a candidate) has a sacred trust to guard his own virtue and maintain it. He has just as sacred a trust to guard that of the young women with whom he associates. The proper and holy association which brings families into the world determined to reach their high destiny is the most satisfying of all the gifts of God, our Father. In this a man and a woman share equally in the work and in the responsibility. In our language it is called marriage, or sealing, for eternity.

The wanton misuse of this privilege, the notion that one can enjoy its gifts without accepting its responsibilities; the mistaken idea that one must, in order to live, test his powers because he has an urge; the deliberate, illicit arousing of the emotions which are a part of this great privilege; all such are the work of Satan. No one ever violated virtue without, in the end, running into the stone wall of being unable to forgive himself.

It is something like a father who gives his boy the family farm. He says, "Use it, don't abuse it — and it will support you well. I've struggled all these years to equip it for you, so now all you have to do is to obey the laws of nature to gain security and happiness." Then he goes on a long vacation.

The boy takes the farm, but he didn't have to fight to get it, so it is not appreciated. He floods out the lower 40, and sets fire to the ripening grain in the upper 10, tips over the tractor into the ditch, and lets the pigs run through the house. He doesn't care!

When the father returns and surveys the wanton damage and sees the contempt with which his gift is received and used, he is hurt — and angry!

To abuse and misuse your privileges given by the Father of us all when you have been given the authority to represent him through the Priesthood is a poor way to show gratitude for the gift. And it can lead to sorrow and life-long regret.

The unwavering observance of its laws, the constant determination to respect girls and to protect them from licentiousness, are goals worthy of a holder of the Aaronic Priesthood. By so doing he best fulfills the hopes his Father holds for him for his eternal growth.

CHAPTER 25 •

RESPECT FOR PARENTS

Nearly every boy in this day is alert to artificial satellites. Few there are who do not know that the moon is a large satellite tied to the earth by the law of gravity, and that it resists the pull of gravitation by its centrifugal force — the speed with which it constantly tries to pull away. The law and the force are in perfect balance — one holds, the other pulls. Each day we read in the newspapers of more and more attempts to put some gigantic rocket into orbit — to get into the same balance as the moon.

The universe is well planned. As long as it pleases the Lord God to have the law obeyed, every star, every world, every satellite will be in orbit, and will stay in orbit. Because of this ordered obedience to the sidereal law the moon was full last night. It will be full again 28 days from now, and 28 days after that. It has been that way for a very long time. This is the order of the universe.

In the past the eternal sacredness of parenthood has been lost. Marriage and parenthood ended at death. In the mistaken notions of men about heaven there was no marriage, and there-fore no families — no fathers and no children. Fatherhood and motherhood are sacred. What is more, they are eternal. They are of the true order of heaven. The revelations bringing into our grasp the principles of eternal marriage, eternal fatherhood and motherhood, the necessity of connecting ourselves in an eternal sealing from father to son clear back to Adam — yes, and as far forward as the earth shall stand — are as much a part of the eternal grandeur of the Lord's plan as is his success in putting the earth in orbit around the sun, and the sun in its turn to revolving around a greater star, carrying with it its collection of planets and their moons.

In the endless chain of fatherhood no one is unimportant. The rules and regulations by which we eventually become sons of God through the Priesthood are tightly bound up in the heavenly order of father to son — so the son gives gratitude to his father and his mother. Giving this to ancestors who are dead is a difficult thing. About all we can do is look them up, find their dates of birth, marriage, death, and then spend a few hours in the Temple in their behalf. But our living parents — the only link between us and our ancestors — are here with us. Some-times their parents (our grandparents) are still here, aged and often crippled with chronic illness. Can we look beyond their aging bodies and see in them the true order of our destiny?

A high-thinking holder of the Priesthood will willingly give not only respect and honor but all he possesses in physical goods, if necessary, to make their declining years memorable because of the happy assistance he gives and the attention he pays to their wants.

Old folk mean a great deal to Latter-day Saints. These have fought the good fight. They have struggled to provide for their children and tried to teach them correct principles. They made sure that your baptism was by correct principle and authority;

so with your confirmation, and your ordination to the Priesthood. Each of your acts in harmony with the gospel has been coached into you by your parents. Now you have a sacred and manly obligation to adopt one more law and one more practice:

> Honor thy father and thy mother: that thy days may be long upon the land which the Lord thy God giveth thee. (Exodus 20:12)

By honor is meant respect and care.

You know you must obey the laws of machines, force, energy and inertia in order to get up an artificial satellite. You know, too, that you don't fight these laws. If you did, you'd get no satellite. In like manner if you do not obey the laws of parenthood, you get no exaltation. No boy holding the Priest-hood, the power that holds our celestial hopes in orbit, will fail to honor his parents, other parents, grandparents, and the aged.

CHAPTER 26 •

PRAYER

The St. George Temple was slowly nearing completion as the faithful workmen added stone block on stone block to its walls. It would soon be high enough to place the roof timbers. So word was sent out that window glass would be needed. This would re-quire $800 in money and a number of wagons, teams of horses, and drivers to freight the glass from the Pacific Coast. The high-way to Los Angeles today follows, most of the way, the old road they used. So volunteers were sought to go on the long and ardu-ous journey. Others were asked to donate money. Finally came the day of departure. The night previous to this the teamsters with their wagons and horses were gathered at the home of Brother David H. Cannon, who was in charge of the project. They were to leave early the next morning. Brother Cannon had only $200 of the expected donations, with nothing more in sight. He debated: Should he admit that he was defeated, call the trip off until a later time? He was worried — in a quandary. Finally he decided not to tell the men the bad news until the next morning. He then went to his room and placed the problem before the Lord in prayer. He asked that the way could open for the glass to be purchased.

Morning came. Brother Cannon arose prepared to face the disappointment of the men. There was a knock on his door. There stood Peter Nielsen, who said he wanted to donate $600. He said that the previous night it was manifested to him that Brother Cannon needed the money. He had saved it for a new house, but this was more important. He had been impressed to come immediately over to St. George in the early morning to give Brother Cannon his savings.

This answer to prayer was miraculous and immediate. The need was urgent — and vital. Not all answers to prayers come quite as rapidly, but one thing is certain: We should ask — we should pray. Nephi said:

> And now, my beloved brethren, I perceive that ye ponder still in your hearts; and it grieveth me that I must speak concerning this thing. For if ye would hearken unto the Spirit which teacheth a man to pray ye yould know that ye must pray; for the evil spirit teacheth not a man to pray, but teacheth him that he must not pray.

> But behold, I say unto you that ye must pray always, and not faint; that ye must not perform anything unto the Lord save in the first place ye shall pray unto the Father in the name of Christ, that he will consecrate thy performance unto thee, that thy perform-ance may be for the welfare of thy soul. (2 Nephi 32:8-9)

If there is one admonition a holder of the Aaronic Priest-hood should heed, it is: Don't be afraid to pray.

I don't refer to the prayers which open and close our meetings, nor to the prayers said in the family, or at meals. These are offered by our folks. They are regular and necessary. But it is the feeling of dependence on the Lord for help in the things you do as a boy each day. There is nothing you do which is unimportant, for each habit you form, the manner in which you tackle a job, the thoroughness with which you prepare for exams, the physical and mental sharpness with which you play basketball — all require help if you are to be successful in the effort. You have been given the gift of the Holy Ghost. He, through his great power, stands ready to shower the gifts upon you if you will receive. But you must think about your needs and the help which can come; then ask for it.

The pioneers understood this principle. Brother Cannon got the money for the glass in the Temple windows. The sea gulls devoured the crickets. Wilford Woodruff went where he was sent by the whisperings — You haven't heard that story, have you? Here it is:

March 1st, 1840, was by birthday; I was thirty-three years of age. It being Sunday, I preached twice during the day to a large assembly in the city hall, in the town of Hanley, and administered the Sacrament to the Saints. In the evening I again met with a large assembly of the Saints and strangers, and while singing the first hymn the spirit of the Lord rested upon me and the voice of God said to me, "This is the last meeting that you will hold with this people for many days." I was astonished at this, as I had many appointments out in that district. When I arose to speak to the people, I told them that it was the last meeting I should hold with them for many days. They were as much astonished as I was. At the close of the meeting four persons came forward for baptism: we went down into the water and baptized them.

In the morning I went in secret before the Lord, and asked Him what was His will concerning me. The answer I received was that I should go to the south; for the Lord had a great work for me to perform there, as many souls were waiting for His word. On the 3rd of March, 1840, in fulfillment of the directions given me, I took coach and rode to Wolverhampton, twenty-six miles, spending the night there. On the morning of the 4th I again took coach, and rode through Dudley, Stourbridge, Stourport, and Worcester, and then walked a number of miles to Mr. John Benbow's, Hill Farm, Castle Frome, Ledbury, Herefordshire. This was a farming country in the south of England, a region where no elder of the Latter-day Saints had visited.

I found Mr. Benbow to be a wealthy farmer, cultivating three hundred acres of land, occupying a good mansion, and having plenty of means. His wife, Jane, had no children. I presented myself to him as a missionary from America, an elder of the Church of Jesus Christ of Latter-day Saints, who had been sent to him by the commandment of God as a messenger of salvation, to preach the gospel of life to him and his household and the inhabitants of the land. He and his wife received me with glad hearts and thanksgiving. It was in the evening when I arrived, having traveled forty-eight miles by coach and on foot during the day, but after receiving refreshments we sat down together, and conversed until two o'clock in the morning. Mr. Benbow and his wife rejoiced greatly at the glad tidings which I brought them.

I also rejoiced greatly at the news Mr. Benbow gave me, that there was a company of men and women — over six hundred in number — who had broken off from the Wesleyan Methodists, and taken the name of United Brethren. They had forty-five preachers among them, and for religious services had chapels and many houses that were licensed according to the law of the land. This body of United Brethren were searching for light and truth, but had gone as far as they could, and were calling upon the Lord continually to open the way before them and send them light and knowledge, that they might know the true way to be saved. When I heard these things I could clearly see why the Lord had commanded me, while in the town of Hanley, to leave that place of labor and go to the south;

for in Herefordshire there was a great harvest-field for gathering many saints into the Kingdom of God. After offering my prayers and thanksgiving to God, I retired to my bed with joy, and slept well until the rising of the sun.

I arose on the morning of the 5th, took breakfast, and told Mr. Benbow I would like to commence my Master's business by preaching the gospel to the people. He had in his mansion a large hall which was licensed for preaching, and he sent word through the neighborhood that an American missionary would preach at his house that evening. As the time drew nigh, many of the neighbors came in, and I preached my first gospel sermon in the house. I also preached at the same place on the following evening, and baptized six persons, including Mr. John Benbow, his wife, and four preachers of the United Brethren. I spent most of the following day in clearing out a pool of water and preparing it for baptizing, as I saw that many would receive that ordinance. I afterwards baptized six hundred persons in that pool of water. (*Life of Wilford Woodruff*, Cowley, pp. 116-117)

Notice that Wilford didn't know exactly where to go — but he went until the spirit led him to the Benbow home.

You are not yet, perhaps, to do miraculous things, or have startling things happen to you. But now is the time to get the habit of asking the Lord about all your affairs and seeking his help. The Prophet Joseph Smith said that he was confused about which church to join. He prayed and got his answer!

President David O. McKay wanted to know the truth also. He dismounted from his horse, got behind a serviceberry bush and asked. His was a delayed answer, but he received it.

In your heart, in secret room or grove, ask the Lord, not once, but many times each day, for help, for guidance, for solution of problems, for aid with work. Soon you'll detect as Wilford

Woodruff detected, the spirit whisperings which will guide you safely through your life.

Amulek gives us the final key to it:

Yea, cry unto him for mercy; for he is mighty to save.

Yea, humble yourselves, and continue in prayer unto him.

Cry unto him when ye are in your fields, yea, over all your flocks.

Cry unto him in your houses, yea, over all your household, both morning, mid-day, and evening.

Yea, cry unto him against the power of your enemies.

Yea, cry unto him against the devil, who is an enemy to all righteousness.

Cry unto him over the crops of your fields, that ye may prosper in them.

Cry over the flocks of your fields, that they may increase.

But this is not all; ye must pour out your souls in your closets, and your sacred places, and in your wilderness.

Yea, and when you do not cry unto the Lord, let your hearts be full, drawn out in prayer unto him continually for your welfare, and also for the welfare of those who are around you. (Alma 34:18-27)

CHAPTER 27

TITHING

Somewhere, sometime, if you are truly going to develop any true value as a servant of the Lord, you must learn that you are as personally responsible for the success of the Lord's purposes as is the President of the Church. This is not to say that you will have to make the same broad decisions as he does, but it does mean that the success of those decisions depends on how you move to support or reject them; how you put your strength into making the Church projects work. You must learn to accept and practice *responsibility*. This is a long word. What does it mean?

Back in 1911 my father had a dozen peach trees on our lot. Most families did in those days. Each summer we spent the time at grandfather's canyon camp at Mountain Dell in Parley's Canyon. And every summer there were few peaches to harvest because, whether green or ripe, the peaches were taken by the boys of the neighborhood. The ripe fruit was eaten and the green peaches used as ammunition in the mock battles of the day. Chief offenders were three boys whose lot abutted our back fence. One summer Father decided that instead of trying to catch the boys and punish them he would try a different tactic. He hired the three neighbor boys to watch the orchard and protect the fruit from other boys. They could take the fruit if they wanted to, but somehow the zest for stealing was gone, for they were responsible for the fruit. They had *responsibility*. We harvested a good crop that fall.

You cannot feel responsible unless you are doing something for the Church. The tasks and assignments given you by the bishop are helpful, but in addition you yourself must feel responsibility. And you can become a part of this responsibility by paying tithes.

The Lord intends to have every nation hear the gospel, and by natural means; that is, he isn't going to perform miracles to get the gospel to South America. Someone must be willing to go there and proclaim it. That isn't a miracle — that is a responsibility. The dead must hear the gospel. They are not where we can reach them, but when they accept the gospel, their baptisms and other ordinances must have been done for them. So we take responsibility to perform the work for the dead.

Going to the Temple — or going to South America on a mission — requires money. Each project must be financed. In order that each could pay his fair share of all the Church responsibilities the Lord gave us the Law of Tithing. There are other reasons — but this is an important one.

You may not have felt *responsible* for the Church as a growing boy, but certainly when you received the Priesthood and began to exercise its authorities there was likely born in you a feeling that you are now truly responsible for its success. Pay your tithing. Take one-tenth of your earnings — your profit if you receive money that way — and show the Lord that you take responsibility for the success of his work.

If you are earning by a wage — you pay one-tenth of the total of that wage.

If you are in business — for example, you are raising a calf, or handling chickens — you pay one-tenth of the amount left after you have paid the bills for feeding and rearing. This is known as the net profit.

What does this money do? Is a dollar your fair share? Yes, if the dollar is one-tenth of an earned or profited ten dollars.

I make a thousand dollars — I pay a hundred.
I make fifty dollars — I pay five.
I make one dollar — I pay ten cents.
I make ten cents — I pay one cent.

And each contribution is equally acceptable to the Lord. Assume that the Church must have fifty million dollars to finance its work. That's a lot of money. I can't give that much, but I can give 10 cents if I earn one dollar. The tithes of the earnings of a million and a half Church members will be far greater than the fifty million which might be needed at the moment.

You will never truly feel as if you belong until you take this responsibility. You will have to do this one voluntarily. It will not be given to you as a definite assignment.

Let's see what we help to do when we pay tithing.

Missionary Work:

The missionary walks up to a door and meets the owner there. He gives him a tract (a pamphlet explaining our beliefs). You bought that tract and put it in the hands of the missionary.

The missionary is released and comes home. You paid your share of his fare home.

The missionary distributes the Book of Mormon for 50 cents. Imagine, a 600 page book for 50 cents! He can do it because you pay for the difference in its real cost and what he sells it for.

The missionary must have a mission headquarters to go to, and from which to receive supervision. Your tithe helps pay for the building, the heat, light, upkeep, and for the supervision.

Temple Work:

Your mother goes to the index bureau to get names cleared for temple work. You keep that bureau open and functioning.

Later she goes to the Temple. Someone has to keep the Temple open, cleaned, repaired, heated. Someone has to help her with the ordinance work. It is you who make it possible.

The Organized Church:

Sunday you will go to the ward. You helped pay for half of the building through your tithes, and for its upkeep. You'll play basketball in the amusement hall a lot more happily if you know that your share of its cost of being there at all has been paid. Every one of the great projects, and the small ones, too, in which the Church is engaged is assisted by the ten cents you pay on each dollar earned.

We have mentioned the practical phases. But there is something else. And this will be your satisfaction. The Lord will give you spiritual blessings which you will learn to crave more than the physical joy you get in giving. This is his promise:

> Bring ye all the tithes into the storehouse, that there may be meat in mine house, and prove me now herewith, saith the Lord of hosts, if I will no open you the windows of heaven, and pour you out a blessing, that there shall not be room enough to receive it.
>
> And I will rebuke the devourer for your sakes, and he shall not destroy the fruits of your ground; neither shall your vine cast the fruit before the time in the field, saith the Lord of hosts.
>
> And all nations shall call you blessed: for ye shall be a delightsome land, saith the Lord of hosts. (Malachi 3:10-12)

CHAPTER 28 •

FASTING

Now that you are a partner in the great plan to exalt the sons of the Lord God, your obedience to the Gospel's laws, ordinances, and practices will make you the recipient of the spiritual blessings. You experience these, often without realizing that they are yours. Sometime, though, you will be able to feel the difference as these blessings come to you, as against when they do not.

You will need to remember that "there is a law, irrevocably decreed in heaven before the foundations of the world, upon which all blessings are predicated—" (Doc. & Cov. 130:20) If you want a blessing you must obey its corresponding law.

Fasting is a means we use to place ourselves in harmony with the Spirit. We fast — we deny ourselves, we give the spiritual part of our natures an opportunity to be more important than the physical part. Nearly always, when prophets have gone before the Lord to ask for information they have fasted first.

We need to be reminded of this necessity or we would likely not fast as often as we should. The monthly fast day reminds us. It also helps us to remember the purpose of that particular fast day. We are asked to remember the poor. Fasting helps us to remember how it feels to be hungry. We don't have much sympathy for others if we are well fed.

This brings us important questions:

How long shall I fast?

How complete should it be?

For the regular monthly fast day to remember the poor, the custom of the Church has been that the fast is for 24 hours —

or for two meals. Instruction has also been given that the fast should be complete—neither food nor water should be taken. So if someone asks you if you should drink water while fasting, the answer is "No." The exception is, of course, the swallow of water and the morsel of bread you partake when the Sacrament is passed.

Other fast days may be held: to pray for the healing of a loved one, to become more humble before delivering a talk, to gain inspiration before making an important decision — each of these fasts has its purpose. It is wise to fast no more than 24 hours for each of these experiences.

Wisdom should rule. A three-year-old child should not be required to fast for 24 hours. Perhaps, under special circum' stances, the time of certain children should be shortened. But you are now old enough. While it is difficult to do the full time, when the time comes that you succeed you will get such satisfaction that you will want to do it that way for the sake of the blessing you will know you received.

Thus saith the Lord:

Also, I give unto you a commandment that ye shall continue in prayer and fasting from this time forth. (Doc. & Cov. 88:76)

CHAPTER 29

SUNDAY

All nations have laws. These they enforce. You disobey civil law at the peril of being locked up in jail.

God our Father has made laws. He gives you freedom to obey or disobey. Rewards follow obedience almost at once. Punishments follow disobediences, but these are often delayed until we assume that they do not exist. Voluntary obedience to the laws of God is the greatest habit you can form.

There have been times when we have thought that we could obtain obedience to keeping the Sabbath day by passing laws prohibiting opening of stores on Sunday. This was recently tried in Utah, but as you know, did not become a law of the state. But it is still a law of God. The fact that a store is open on Sunday does not give you license to go into that store. Go downtown on Sunday. Most stores are closed. But a few are open. They are open because the storekeepers have learned that people at home for a day of rest more often treat it as a holiday and buy these pleasant-tasting items more on that day.

But suppose you didn't buy these things on Sunday. The store and drive-in would close for lack of customers. So in a very real sense every time you stop in and buy on Sunday you are breaking the Sabbath, and giving excuse for the store owner to break it. Most boys do it. So do most girls.

You say, why do they break the Sabbath? Why don't they close? They break it because they want the profit from the money you spend on Sunday when you break it. It isn't a very good reason, but it is a very real reason. So if you keep holy the Sabbath day, you will make it entirely unnecessary to pass a law in the state legislature forcing stores to close. Of course the law should be there anyhow because some won't close unless forced to.

Then there are the moving-picture theaters. They run on Sunday. But if no one went in on Sunday they'd close, too.

A good rule to make is that you will spend no money on Sunday. That will go a long way toward helping you to resist Sunday amusements.

Another good rule to follow is that you will wear your best clothes all day and not change into every-day wear. That will help, too.

But there is no rule that you can make that will give you the right spirit for the observance of the Sabbath day like your feeling the desire and the resolution to obey the instruction given by the Lord to the Prophet Joseph Smith. This is absolute and final and is the real test as to whether or not the Priesthood is in your heart and soul, and obedience to its authority is your desire. This is the Lord speaking:

> And that thou mayest more fully keep thyself unspotted from the world, thou shalt go to the house of prayer and offer up thy sacraments upon my holy day;
>
> For verily this is a day appointed unto you to rest from your labors, and to pay thy devotions unto the Most High; . . .
>
> But remember that on this, the Lord's day, thou shalt offer thine oblations and thy sacraments unto the Most High . . .
>
> And on this day thou shalt do none other thing, only let thy food be prepared with singleness of heart, that thy fasting may be perfect, or, in other words, that thy joy may be full . . .
>
> Verily I say, that inasmuch as ye do this, the fullness of the earth is yours . . . (Doc. & Cov. 59:9-10, 12-13, 16)

What then *exactly* may you do on Sunday? What you do on Sunday will be a good measure of how much you have in you the spirit of the Lord. You will know very well what not to do if you listen to the still small voice of the spirit which you as a Priesthood bearer are trying to learn how to hear.

Just to show you that some of it is up to you, this is how the Lord looks at going into detail. He knows that you will know if you try to do what is right, so he left it up to you. He said:

For behold, it is not meet that I should command in all things; for he that is compelled in all things, the same is a slothful and not a wise servant; wherefore he receiveth no reward.

Verily I say, men should be anxiously engaged in a good cause, and do many things of their own free will, and bring to pass much righteousness;

For the power is in them, wherein they are agents unto themselves. And inasmuch as men do good they shall in nowise lose their reward.

But he that doeth not anything until he is commanded, and receiveth a commandment with doubtful heart, and keepeth it with slothfulness, the same is damned.

Who am I that made man, saith the Lord, that will hold him guiltless that obeys not my commandments? (Doc. & Cov. 58:26-30)

CHAPTER 30 •

SEMINARIES

All members of the Church are converts. Some are born in the Church and are baptized at the age of eight. They are familiar with the Church and its procedures because they grew up in it, but they are not necessarily familiar with the doctrines or with the scriptures which explain them. They will need to learn the doctrine and accept it if they stay in the Church. They become converted principle by principle. Others join the Church after investigation of its principles and doctrine, and are the converts of whom we ordinarily speak. No matter in which way you became a member, you must accept the doctrine if you are to be a Latter-day Saint.

The Church provides auxiliary organizations which are designed to give each person a well-rounded knowledge of the doctrine. The courses of study and of practice are graded to teach you at your age the particular material you are able to understand. So you have the Sunday School. To practice ethical living you go to Primary and, later, to Mutual. These fine organizations assist you from your kindergarten years to adult-hood. The Priesthood quorum to which you belong carries you farther with an approach slightly different, for it gives you experience in the actual government of the Church.

When you enter high school, however, you come to an age when the viewpoint of the world is pressed upon you. Questions arise in your mind which are disturbing to you. Here the semi-naries are provided to serve you. They offer classes five days a week, where the other helping auxiliaries are able to meet only once a week. The teachers, having made this their life's work, are well trained both in teaching and in knowledge. Here you can get a thorough knowledge of the standard works of the Church — the scriptures — the revelations.

Then, too, you are able to meet like-minded young folk who are, as are you, eager to learn of, and to do for, the Lord. The classes are usually held in buildings adjacent to high schools in those parts of the Church where there are enough LDS students in the schools. In other places parents and teachers work out a system wherein early, before school, classes are conducted. Here a real test of loyalty is made, for the student has to arise early indeed to get to a seven a.m. class.

A very high percentage of seminary students become thor-ough converts to the gospel and complete all of the ordinances. They are later sealed in marriage in the Temple, in most instances.

I myself took seminary at a time when it was first started. The first classes were held with the students of Granite High School in a nearby home. But so successful was it that for the second year a building was constructed directly opposite the school. I spent four happy years there. The teachers were pro-found men. They could give insight into what I needed to know. I received a good first-hand knowledge of the Bible, the Book of Mormon, and the Doctrine and Covenants. They didn't teach the Pearl of Great Price. That is interesting as I look back, for I didn't really know that book until I was very much older. It would have been the same had I not studied the other three in seminary. I have been grateful ever since that I went there, for it has been to my entire advantage.

The college institutes serve the same purpose for college students. These are, in addition, designed to give social life on a high plane to the students, who, often living away from home, discover that the institute gives to college some of their home atmosphere.

Conversion to the gospel must come to each person. Each doctrine, each principle, must be known and accepted — and lived — if you are to honor the Priesthood. You were given the Priesthood without having much knowledge, but it was not intended that you should remain ignorant of the gospel. You must gain knowledge of doctrine to honor the great gift of the Priesthood. There is no better way to do this than to take advan' tage of the seminaries and the college institutes. Don't miss the opportunity. You'll never be sorry.

CHAPTER 31 •

THE CHURCH OR
THE WORLD

Somewhere along the trail you will come to a side road. The main trail leads on to manhood, to faithful and joyful service in the Church, to happy marriage and satisfying family life. The side road leads to a manhood of worldly things, fascinating, enticing on the surface; but having no real depth of meaning. Sometimes young men get on this road without realizing they have detoured. Here are some signs by which you may know when you are on the side road:

1. You'll wake up Sunday morning and decide that you'd rather sleep than go to Church!

2. You'll go to the drugstore or confectionary and stop to

hob-nob with the boys who hang around the corner. Soon it will seem more fun to be there than in Church.

3. One of your friends may have a car, or you may have one yourself. Getting out on the highway, or hot-rodding through town on Sunday stripped to the waist is exciting. The temptation to appear a big shot seems irresistible.

4. You and your friends find pleasure in late movies on Sunday. They are certainly more exciting than Sacrament meeting.

5. You may be led to try cigarettes or a can of beer; or be told that to prove that you really are a man, you must try stronger drink.

All of these and many more like them lead you away from your goal of eternal life — and they give you false ideas of the meaning of pleasure and happiness.

Out in a town just over the Nevada line there is a sign on a building inviting you to come in and "have fun." But the "fun" to be had consists of a long row of slot machines, and some tables at which smooth, hard-faced men invite you to gamble with them. Drinking liquor is a part of the "fun." So a bar is close by. Scantily-clad girls bring drinks quickly so a person can have more "fun."

Any boy who has had any experience at all in the real pleasures of social life in the Church can see through these thin attempts to entice him away. For the fun there is not fun at all. It is excitement, but it isn't fun. It never was; it never will be.

Elder Richard L. Evans once heard a great man speak about the problems of our times. Real thinking men are worried about the vices of men — young and old. They have read history. They know where vice leads a nation. Indulgence in it leads to ruin. The man asked in one sentence a question. This question sums up the whole problem which we face:

"Are we going to be a part of the problem or a part of the answers?"

CHAPTER 32 •

PRIESTHOOD POWER

It is important that you learn more about the power of the Priesthood. For it, in its full use, is the means by which the Lord created the earth. You are going to learn much about it in your lifetime.

You have known about the power to heal the sick. Did you know that in the beginnings of Nauvoo illness struck down the Saints in such numbers that most of them were sick and many dying? So great was this affliction that the Prophet was moved to invoke the power of the Priesthood. Wilford Woodruff described it as follows:

> In consequence of the persecutions of the Saints in Missouri, and the exposures to which they were subjected,

many of them were taken sick soon after their arrival at Commerce, afterwards called Nauvoo; and as there was but a small number of dwellings for them to occupy, Joseph had filled his house and tent with them, and through constantly attending to their wants, he soon fell sick himself. After being confined to his house several days, and while meditating upon his situation, he had a great desire to attend to the duties of his office. On the morning of the 22nd of July, 1839, he arose from his bed and commenced to administer to the sick in his own house and door-yard, and he commanded them in the name of the Lord Jesus Christ to arise and be made whole; and the sick were healed upon every side of him.

Many lay sick along the bank of the river; Joseph walked along up to the lower stone house, occupied by Sidney Rigdon, and he healed all the sick that lay in his path. Among the number was Henry G. Sherwood, who was nigh unto death. Joseph stood in the door of his tent and commanded him in the name of Jesus Christ to arise and come out of his tent, and he obeyed him and was healed. Brother Benjamin Brown and his family also lay sick, the former appearing to be in a dying condition. Joseph healed them in the name of the Lord. After healing all that lay sick upon the bank of the river as far as the stone house, he called upon Elder Kimball and some others to accompany him across the river to visit the sick at Montrose. Many of the Saints were living at the old military barracks. Among the number were several of the Twelve. On his arrival the first house he visited was that occupied by Elder Brigham Young, the President of the Quorum of the Twelve, who lay sick. Joseph healed him, then he arose and accompanied the Prophet on his visit to others who were in the same condition. They visited Elder Wilford Woodruff, also Elders Orson Pratt, and John Taylor, all of whom were living in Montrose. They also accompanied him.

The next place they visited was the home of Elijah Fordham, who was supposed to be about breathing his last. When the company entered the room, the Prophet of God walked up to the dying man and took hold of his right hand and spoke to him; but Brother Fordham was unable to speak, his eyes were set in his head like glass, and he seemed entirely unconscious of all around him. Joseph held his hand and looked into his eyes in silence for a length of time. A change in the countenance of Brother Fordham was soon perceptible to all present. His sight returned, and upon Joseph asking him if he knew him, he, in a low whisper, answered "Yes." Joseph asked him if he had faith to be healed. He answered, "I fear it is too late; if you had come sooner I think I would have been healed." The Prophet said, "Do you believe in Jesus Christ?" He answered in a feeble voice, "I do." Joseph then stood erect, still holding his hand in silence several moments; then he spoke in a very loud voice, saying, "Brother Fordham, I command you, in the name of Jesus Christ, to arise from this bed and be made whole." His voice was like the voice of God, and not of man. It seemed as though the house shook to its very foundations. Brother Fordham arose from his bed, and was immediately made whole. His feet were bound in poultices which he kicked off; then putting on his clothes he ate a bowl of bread and milk and followed the Prophet into the street.

The company next visited Brother Joseph Bates Noble, who lay very sick. He also was healed by the Prophet. By this time the wicked became alarmed and followed the company into Brother Noble's house. After Noble was healed, all kneeled down to pray. Brother Fordham was mouth, and while praying he fell to the floor. The Prophet arose, and on looking around he saw quite a number of unbelievers in the house. whom he ordered out. When the room was cleared of the wicked, Brother Fordham came to and finished his prayer.

After healing the sick in Montrose, all the company followed Joseph to the bank of the river, where he was going to take the boat to return home. While waiting for the boat, a man from the West, who had seen that the sick and dying were healed, asked Joseph if he would not go to his house and heal two of his children who were very sick. They were twins and were three months old. Joseph told the man he could not go, but he would send someone to heal them. He told Elder Woodruff to go with the man and heal his children. At the same time he took from his pocket a silk bandanna handkerchief, and gave to Brother Woodruff, telling him to wipe the faces of the children with it, and they should be healed; and remarked at the same time: "As long as you keep the handkerchief it shall remain a league between you and me." Elder Woodruff did as he was commanded, and the children were healed, and he keeps the handkerchief to this day.

There were many sick whom Joseph could not visit, so he counseled the Twelve to go and visit and heal them, and many were healed under their hands. On the day following that upon which the above-described events took place, Joseph sent Elders George A. and Don Carlos Smith up the river to heal the sick. They went up as far as Ebenezer Robinson's — one or two miles — and did as they were commanded, and the sick were healed. (Footnote, *History of the Church*, Vol. IV, pp. 3-5)

Its power has been used to stop evil men in their tracks. Parley P. Pratt was present on one occasion:

In one of those tedious nights we had lain as if in sleep till the hour of midnight had passed, and our ears and hearts had been pained, while we had listened for hours to the obscene jests, the horrid oaths, the dreadful blasphemies and filthy language of our guards, Colonel Price at their head, as they recounted to each other their deeds of rapine, murder, robbery, etc., which they had committed among the "Mormons" while at Far West and vicinity. They even boasted of defiling by force wives, daughters, and virgins, and of shooting or dashing out the brains of men, women and children.

I had listened till I became so disgusted, shocked, horrified, and so filled with the spirit of indignant justice that I could scarcely refrain from rising upon my feet and rebuking the guards; but had said nothing to Joseph, or anyone else, although I lay next to him and knew he was awake. On a sudden he arose to his feet, and spoke in a voice of thunder, or as the roaring lion, uttering, as near as I can recollect, the following words:

"SILENCE, ye fiends of the infernal pit. In the name of Jesus Christ I rebuke you, and command you to be still; I will not live another minute and hear such language. Cease such talk, or you or I die THIS INSTANT!"

He ceased to speak. He stood erect in terrible majesty. Chained, and without a weapon; calm, unruffled, and dignified as an angel, he looked upon the quailing guards, whose weapons were lowered or dropped to the ground; whose knees smote together, and who, shrinking into a corner, or crouching at his feet, begged his pardon, and remained quiet till a change of guards. (*Autobiography of Parley P. Pratt,* pp. 210-211)

David W. Patten, an early apostle and the first martyr to fall defending the Church, was:

. . . taken by an armed mob under a United States warrant. When he was surrounded by about forty such men who were acting under the garb of law, and who forbade him to say one word in his own defense, he arose in the power of God and held them fast to their seats until he had addressed them for about one-half hour. He told them that they were cowards, rascals, and villains, and proved it to them and they had not the power to harm one hair of his head, and they let him and Warren Parrish go free. (*Life of Wilford Woodruff,* Cowley, pp. 378-379)

No man holding such power would boast. He would be more than ever humble and careful. But when invoked under the inspiration of the Holy Ghost this power is irresistible whether in rebuke or in succor of the helpless.

You hold a sacred thing, a wonderful thing when you hold the Priesthood. You will discover that there is no limit to the strength you will get from it when you are in the service of the Lord. And there is something terrible in its power when it is used to rebuke.

No one should invoke it except in righteousness as inspired by the Holy Ghost. In your work as a holder of the Aaronic Priesthood, so live that you can receive the Melchizedek Priest-hood. Then live worthy of that and you will truly find your destiny fulfilled.

Now go forward and do your best to be worthy of its blessings.